Football's Even-Front Defense

Football's Even-Front Defense

Jerry Howell

Parker Publishing Co., Inc. • West Nyack, N.Y.

© 1983, *by*

Parker Publishing Company, Inc.

West Nyack, N.Y.

Library of Congress Cataloging in Publication Data

Howell, Jerry.
    Football's even-front defense.

    Includes index.
    1. Football—Defense. 2. Football—Coaching.
I. Title.
GV951.18.H68   1983   796.332′2   83-6250
ISBN 0-13-324079-7

Printed in the United States of America

HOW THE EVEN FRONT
WILL HELP YOU

Ask ANY COACH ON ANY LEVEL what single factor contributes most to winning football games—his resounding answer will be DEFENSE.

The ability to control the opponent's offense is a must which allows you to set the tempo of the game. With the even defense you utilize the unique talents of your entire team to their fullest in developing your offensive and kicking games. In short, a strong defense lays the foundation for the rest of your game.

All over the country a trend has developed as teams are changing from the 50 or odd fronts popular in the 1970's to the new look—Even defensive fronts of the '80s.

During the 1970's, the 50 front was used by every top-20 team except Penn State. By 1981, traditional defensive powers such as Texas, USC, Washington, Notre Dame, Georgia, Pitt, Texas A&M, Mississippi State and many others had begun to use some form of the even defensive front. The flexibility of the college 4-3 has allowed many teams to retain the successful components of their 50 package within their new look and also utilize the additional strengths of the college 4-3.

The college 4-3 is the defensive system that is leading the switch in defensive philosophies. It offers so many possible combinations that the defensive game plan can be adjusted from week to week without radically altering the entire defensive package.

7

Even fronts are more effective against the run and allow defenses to stunt and attack the offense with greater success. The concepts, principles, and schemes detailed in this book provide a package that will be effective no matter what type of talent is available. Therefore, the size and athletic ability of a lineman are not the factors they were in the 50 front.

The even front allows for a balanced pass rush of at least 4 people. The front can be easily adjusted to create optimal pass rush responsibilities while maintaining solid underneath coverage and perimeter defense.

By utilizing the even defensive concept, the underdog can continually attack the defense from a variety of angles that will create confusion in the offense. The resulting chaos will demoralize the opponent, thereby giving you the little edge that makes the difference between winning and losing.

Jerry Howell

CONTENTS

Chapter 1

WHY USE THE EVEN FRONT? 19

Chapter 2

AGILITY AND REACTION—WHAT
DEFENSE IS ALL ABOUT 27

Chapter 3

TACKLING FUNDAMENTALS
AND TECHNIQUES 43

Chapter 4

DEFENSIVE LINE FUNDAMENTALS
AND TECHNIQUES 63

Chapter 7

BREAKDOWN OF RULES, ASSIGNMENTS, COVERAGES, STUNTS AND TECHNIQUES TO BE USED WITH EVEN FRONTS

Chapter 8

PRACTICE AND SCOUTING SUMMARY—TOTAL PRACTICE PREPARATION FOR THE YEAR-AROUND PROGRAM 183

FOOTBALL DRILL DIAGRAM KEY

O—Player
R—Runner—Offensive Player—Right Foot
T—Tackler—Defensive Player
◨—Center
C—Coach
M—Manager
☐—Bag
△—Cone
▣—▣—▣—Sled
B—Ball
L—Left Foot

FOOTBALL DEFENSIVE PERSONNEL KEY

O—Offensive Player
C—Cornerback—WC/Weak Corner—SC/Strong Corner
F—Free Safety
K—Kat—Strong Safety
M—Mike Backer—Middle/Inside
S—Sam Backer—Strong Side
W—Willie Backer—Weak Side
V—Victors
T—Defensive Tackle
E—Defensive End
G—Defensive Guard

Football's
Even-Front
Defense

Chapter 1

WHY USE THE EVEN FRONT?

IT'S THE DEFENSE THAT WINS FOOTBALL GAMES. All successful football teams play good defensive football. In order for you to be successful each year, you must have a good defensive game plan.

We believe in the even front as our basic defense. This defense will allow you great flexibility in your attack against the opponents. Yours will not be a passive type of defense, but rather an aggressive, penetrating defense. You will take the fight to them. You will be the aggressors, presenting a multiple of problems for the offense.

Many offenses are predicated on grinding out yardage against passive defenses. By stunting and penetrating, you will get offenses into 2nd-and-long, and 3rd-and-long situations. By studying tendencies from films and scouting reports you will take away their best plays and force them to use low-percentage plays. Yours is not a gambling defense, but rather you will attack in some areas and help each other with a coordinated defensive package.

Causing turnovers will be a major part of your defensive attack. By being a hard-hitting, aggressive, gang-tackling unit, you will intimidate the offenses into giving the football up and take away their will to win.

Each player has the responsibility to know your total defense and his individual assignments. It is only his ability to combine this knowledge with physical fitness and the right frame of mind that will give you the perfection of execution needed for victory.

19

This defense is not a complicated one, but rather one you can easily learn and then practice for top execution. The wide range of defensive fronts available is helpful only if we out-execute our opponent.

You must always take pride in whatever you are doing. With hard work and hustling, your season will be successful and something to be proud of.

Why use the even front you ask? After all, most teams are using the Oakie front. Most people copy what the "bigs" find successful. The 50 front was used by most of the top ten Division I schools in the sixties and seventies. Therefore, everyone tried to copy those people. Unfortunately, many of you found that Alabama and Oklahoma had much better nose guards than you could produce year in and year out. If you are lucky enough to have the big studs every year, you also found the 50 lacking in stunt possibilities. The 50 is primarily a reading defense. Many of you can't play a reading defense because of size limitations. Others like us just don't believe in the 50 and are waiting to see what the other guy does. Our philosophy has always been one of attacking. A defense must take chances. The concept of attacking is based on forcing the offense into offensive situations they don't normally practice. If you force a loss on first down, then the offense is trying to call a 2nd-and-12 play. Very few people practice plays for this type of situation. Therefore, we can get into our best contain defense for what we feel will be their 2nd-and-12 play. The advantage now shifts to the defense. The defense is on the offense, having forced its opponent to run plays that are high risk in nature.

Good nose guards are probably the hardest people to develop. At the high school level, you may not always have that kind of material to work with. Also, your tackles have to be the types of people who handle the double-team, shed blocks and find the ball. In the even front, they can be smaller people whose main responsibility is to keep people off the linebackers or penetrate quickly into the backfield. With the even front, the linebackers don't usually have an offensive man right across from them, whom they have to fight while they're reading the backs' action.

Everything comes down to a matter of philosophy. If you have smaller, quick people and feel that you can't sit back and read, then the even front is your answer. We firmly believe that in order to have a successful defense you must force the offense out of its rhythm. This requires slants and crossing actions by the line and combination stunts involving the whole front. We also believe that more teams will have a more effective running game than their pass offense. The even front seems to be stronger against the run. Therefore, by using this approach we attack their strong point and force most people to beat us with the weakest part of their attack.

A strong defense not only demoralizes the opposition by its hard hitting tactics, but also gives a tremendous lift to its own offense by giving the ball to them in good scoring position. Many teams whose offenses have been stopped won the games with the touchdowns scored by the defense. One of the main reasons for upsets in football is that the favorite team fails to score when it has the opportunity to do so, and the underdog capitalizes on a "break" and wins the game. The bottom line is simply, defense wins football games, offense entertains the fans.

OBJECTIVES OF DEFENSIVE FOOTBALL

To Prevent the Easy Touchdown

While the obvious basic objective of defensive football is to keep the opposition from scoring, a more functional objective of defensive play is to prevent the opposition from scoring the easy touchdown via a long pass or a long run. Make your opponent earn every point it scores the hard way.

To Obtain Possession of the Football

A second objective of defensive play is to obtain possession of the football. The defensive team must gain possession of the ball by holding the opponent for downs, forcing a punt, intercepting a pass, recovering a fumble or recovering a blocked punt. Turnovers, no matter where they are forced, will turn the offense on.

To Score

The third objective of defensive play is to score. The defense can score on a punt return, on an intercepted pass, by advancing a blocked punt, by recovering a fumble in the end zone (or, under high school rules, by advancing any fumbled ball for a score), and by forcing the offense to give up a safety.

Defense Consists of Two Coordinated Units

In attempting to realize these three objectives of defensive football, several factors must be considered. In order for any defensive alignment to be sound, the personnel must be deployed in such a manner that the defense is one of depth as well as width, and you must be able to defend against both the run and pass at the same time. While there are many different defensive alignments, a sound defense consists of both a front unit of players on or near the line of scrimmage, and a containing unit or perimeter of players. The number of players in each unit will vary, depending upon the deployment of the defensive personnel, their duties and responsibilities. They will be governed by the tactical situation on each play.

The front unit. In addition to the general objectives of defensive play mentioned already, the methods of obtaining possession of the ball are for the front unit to force a fumble, or force the opposition to surrender the ball on downs. The front unit can also cause interceptions by forcing the passer to throw the ball quickly or to release it at a higher arc so that its trajectory is higher and longer, giving the players in the perimeter unit a better opportunity to intercept the pass. The front unit cannot permit the opposition to retain possession of the football for an extended series of downs, especially in the four-down zone part of the field, since the opposition increases its chances of scoring 25 percent after it reaches this area of play.

Excluding the remaining factors in the tactical situation other than down, distance and position on the field, when the opposition has the ball back in its own territory in the three-down zone part of the field in a first-and-ten situation, it is good defensive play if the offensive gain is held to 3 yards. If the opposition runs the ball two more times and comes up with a fourth-and-one situation, in the three-down zone they will, in all probability, still punt the football on fourth down. Any yardage a team makes in defensive territory which does not get it out past its own 40-yard line is of little value. Even if the offensive team should make the first down, or several consecutive first downs from deep in its own territory, it is difficult to keep a sustained drive going on the ground by grinding out the necessary yardage. The odds favor the defenders that the offensive team will make a mechanical error, such as, a fumble, miss a block, hit the wrong hole, or be penalized, which causes the drive to falter, and they are forced to give up the football to the defense. Offenses get the ball 8 to 12 times a game and they will turn the ball over 50 to 75 percent of the time on their own mistakes, if the defense doesn't make a mistake. The front unit must maintain pressure on the opposition, however, and both units must eliminate the long pass or run for the easy touchdown in order to be sound defensively. This can be achieved by attacking from the even front.

The perimeter unit. The objectives of the perimeter unit are also the same as the three objectives of defensive football mentioned previously, in addition to containing the offensive play. The defensive perimeter may be thought of, and has been referred to, as the last-wall defense. This is one that will bend but will not permit the ball carrier to break through it for the easy touchdown. In the secondary, the three deep men and normally the ends are the rim men in the defensive perimeter, with the ball as the hub of the wheel. The twin safeties and the corner or wingmen are the rim of the defensive perimeter. As the football moves, the rim or defensive perimeter should stay intact and revolve with the football. The objective of the perimeter unit is to keep all of the offensive operations within the rim of the perimeter, which will enable the interior men to pursue and gang-tackle. The secondary men in the perimeter unit go on the assumption that every play is a pass until they read run or see the ball pass the line of scrimmage. These players should make fewer errors with only one pattern of play, and be able to prevent the easy touchdown—which is the first objective of defensive football.

PRINCIPLES OF DEFENSIVE FOOTBALL

In order to realize the objectives of defensive football, the following principles must be taught, and practiced frequently:

1. Build positive defensive morale.
2. The proper angle of pursuit is a must.
3. Gang-tackling is essential.
4. Sound pass defense.
5. Stop the easy score or long gain.

Building Defensive Morale

The importance of pride and morale in football cannot be stressed enough. Relevant to defensive play, a coach should try to develop a positive attitude toward realizing these major objectives. The scoring odds favor the defense, as was cited previously. Therefore, it is advisable to remind the players about the offensive-defense, and scoring while on defense. How many points did the defense score? How many fumbles were recovered by the defensive team? How many passes did the defense intercept? How many times did the defense get the ball for the offense in scoring position? How many goal-line stands killed your opponent's morale?

Interceptions nullify completions. In building defensive morale, two points of view should be cultivated toward the opposition's passing game. A pass is an opportunity and an invitation for the defense to intercept and gain possession of the ball. Second, conceding the point that there is no defense against the perfectly thrown pass and that your opponent will probably complete a number of passes inside the defensive perimeter, still one interception will nullify a number of completions. Defensive morale means maintaining confidence and not panicking when the opposition completes several passes. The next pass will be the interception.

Opposition must earn yardage. Positive morale is built by developing the concept that the closer the opposition gets to the goal line, the more difficult it becomes for them to score. The advantage is with the defense since it has less territory to cover. Offensive ends and backs cannot get behind the defensive secondary.

If the opposition is forced to punt on fourth down, especially from deep in its own territory, the advantage is with the defense. The latter has the opportunity now either to block the punt or to set up the return. If successfully executed, either tactic can produce a score for the defensive team. If neither is successful, at least the defensive team has accomplished an objective in forcing the opposition to give up possession of the football.

Morale is built by developing the concept that nothing is given to the opposition easily—they must earn it. Everything the offense gains is earned the hard way. Punish the opposition physically on every play.

Communication is a must. Defensive morale is built by having the players talk and communicate with each other. When the opposition attempts to pass, all defensive players should shout, "Pass!"; on an interception, "Bingo!"; on a fumble or blocked kick, "Ball!"; on the obvious running play, "Sweep!" "Reverse!" "Trap!" etc. It is very important for the defensive secondary to communicate with each other by calling out, "My man!" "I've got him!" "End across!" "You take him!" and "Switch!"

Proper Angle of Pursuit Is a Must

The proper angle of pursuit is nothing more than getting to the spot where you are going to make the tackle. We feel this is probably the most important factor in defensive football today. What good is it if you have good tacklers but they lack team quickness and cannot get to the spot where they need to be in order to make the tackle? A defensive man may be blocked, but a good defensive player never stays blocked. He should recover as quickly as possible, react to the ball, and begin his proper angle of pursuit. There is some angle that every man on the defensive team can take on the ball carrier. If a defensive player starts his pursuit at the wrong angle, he immediately eliminates himself.

Gang Tackling Is Number One

Defensive people must get excited and play with reckless abandon. Proper and comprehensive scouting techniques, to secure pertinent information, generally will reveal offensive tendencies. This is especially true in high school football where a quarterback or his coach will follow a particular pattern or sequence in long and short yardage situations, in the Scoring Zone, and when trying to get the football out of the Danger Zone. Such factors do contribute to rapid play recognition, build defensive morale, and aid in team pursuit for gang tackling. If the opposition counters by changing its offensive attack, the advantage lies with the defense as the offense has been forced to run something other than its favorite plays and passes. As stated earlier, we want at least three people on the ball carrier and six within three steps. No one just watches or ever gives up.

Good Pass Defense Is Important

Pass defense is undoubtedly the most important phase of defensive football, particularly at the college level. It is difficult to teach, and requires a great deal of time and practice. Pass defense has four important phases:

1. Rushing the passer aggressively.
2. Delaying eligible receivers at or near the line of scrimmage.
3. Secondary pass coverage.
4. Interception of the pass or tackling the receiver.

Rushing the passer aggressively. In order for the defensive men to reach the passer, they must rid themselves of offensive blockers. Many times defensive players try to rush through offensive blockers. Unless they are physically stronger than their opponents, they will not be able to rush through them. The defensive men should use one of at least four pass rush techniques that they have been taught. Unless they have inside containment responsibility, they must force to the outside. In applying pressure on the passer, it is essential that the defensive players rush aggressively, proceeding through their assigned areas of responsibility. The number of men rushing the passer will vary, depending upon the tactical situation and the philosophy of the coach.

Never Allow the Long T.D. or Gain

What can you say here? The long T.D. or gain fires your opponent up, and makes it very hard for your offense to bounce back. You have given them the extra man they needed (Mr. Momentum). Never let that happen if at all possible.

The even defensive front may not be the answer to everyone's defensive problems. But, we feel that too many programs follow national trends without really evaluating the needs and capabilities of their own programs and athletes. This material provides an in-depth study of the uses and strengths of the even fronts in defensive football.

Chapter 2

AGILITY AND REACTION—
WHAT DEFENSE IS ALL ABOUT

THE TRUE MEASURE OF DEFENSIVE FOOTBALL SPEED is quickness and ability to react to the ball, and not necessarily how fast a player can run 50-100 yards. Movement, in football, refers to speed, quickness and agility. The latter two are more important than speed, although lacking any of the three assets will limit the progress of any player. Some athletes are born with a feel for the ball; it can't be taught, but quickness and agility can be improved.

Thinking of agility and reaction as "a physical and mental response to a stimulus," the development of body control, agility and the ability to react quickly and accurately is as important as the proper development of defensive fundamentals. Without these skills, a player will not be able to execute the necessary fundamentals, and he will not be able to control his opponent.

Reaction drills may be used to develop both agility and reaction, whereas simple agility drills are limited in value unless a stimulus is added, along with the teaching of mobility, in order to secure a desired reaction. We suggest that you seldom employ drills that teach only agility, unless that particular agility is also a technique or a fundamental. A limited number of agility and reaction drills will be presented in this chapter, some of which are superior for improving reaction time and developing coordination and agility. These are drills that many of you already use, and most of you can add one or two new ones to the list. They are not presented in a progressive order of importance; you can mix them to meet your needs.

Some drills in Chapters 4, 5, 6 can also be used with agility drills. You may also need to redesign some of these drills to fit your situation and the ability level of your athletes.

Included in the agility-reaction drills are tumbling drills, which develop the ability to control one's body in flight, as well as teach a player how to fall and roll without being injured.

AGILITY AND REACTION DRILLS

There are numerous agility and reaction drills and each drill has variations. Our objective is not to present an infinite number of drills, although many of these may be revised for additional drills. Simple agility drills will be presented first, then reaction drills. Several agility-reaction techniques or fundamentals (drills) will be included. The following drills may be used to develop agility and/or reaction:

1. High Stepper or Toe Dance Drill

Purpose: To develop body balance and agility, and to stretch and loosen the muscles during warm-up.

Procedure: Straddling a line and facing the opposite side of the field, players follow one another across the width of the field—jogging with high-knee action, stretching out the legs, crossing back and forth over the line, landing on the toes, getting torsion in the hips, and exaggerating the natural swing of the arms.

Coaching Points: Emphasize high-knee action and hip movement, not speed. When landing on the toes, the right foot should alight on the left side of the line and the left foot on the right side of the line. Follow up with the Carioca Drill.

2. Carioca or Grapevine Drill (Figure 2-1)

Purpose: To develop body balance, agility, coordination, quickness, and to stretch and loosen the muscles during warm-up.

Procedure: Players stand on lines, facing one end zone. When going left, the player steps laterally with his left foot, crosses over with his right foot in front, steps laterally with his left, crosses right foot behind left, and repeats—staying on the line for the specified distance. Coming back on the line, player works to his right, steps laterally with right foot, crosses over with left in front, right laterally, left behind, etc. The palms and forearms are carried parallel with the ground and player exaggerates natural arm and shoulder movements.

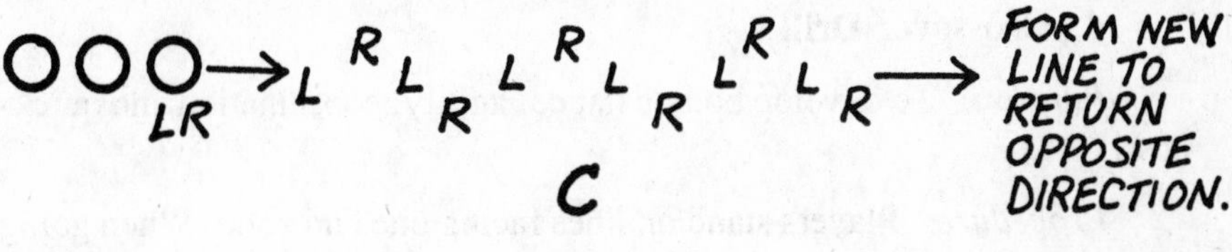

Figure 2-1

Coaching Points: Emphasize exaggerated hip swing, trying to get a rhythmical movement (like the "carioca") rather than a mechanical movement. Increase speed gradually, emphasizing short choppy steps and quick movements.

3. Straddle Drill (Figure 2-2)

Purpose: To develop body balance, agility, coordination, quickness, and to stretch and loosen the muscles during warm-up.

Procedure: Same as for (2)—Carioca or Grapevine Drill—players stand on lines facing one end zone, feet parallel but staggered so that heel of one foot (right) is in front of line, and toe of opposite foot (left) is behind the line. When going left, player jumps laterally, just enough to clear the ground, and reverses position of feet so that left is forward and right is behind the line, repeating movement for the specified distance. Coming back, working right, the player's first movement is laterally to his right, and reversing his feet in a straddle position each time he clears the ground.

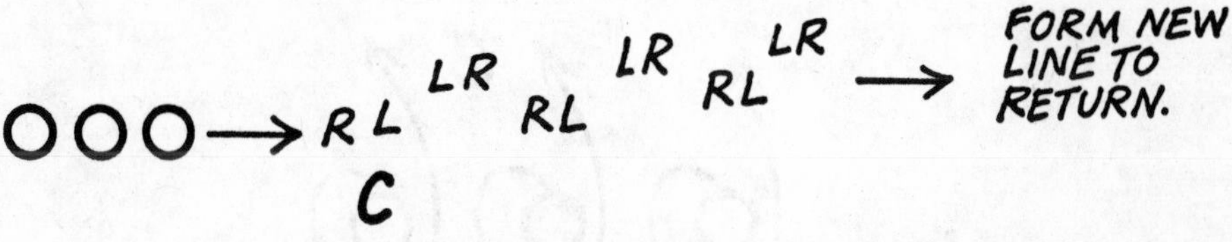

Figure 2-2

Coaching Points: When players first do the drill the straddle will be extended. The objective is to move the feet quickly, taking short choppy steps, landing on the balls of the feet. Emphasize quickness and speed, permitting the player to turn his body so that he is actually making about one-eighth of a turn each time he reverses the position of his feet.

4. Crossover Drill

Purpose: To develop body balance, agility, coordination and quickness.

Procedure: Players stand on lines facing one end zone. When going left, player steps laterally with left foot, crosses over in front with the right foot, left laterally, crosses over in front with the right, etc. He does not alternate crossing over in front, and then behind, with the off foot as in Carioca Drill. The shoulders are kept parallel with the line, and the arms and hands are extended away from in front of the body in a ward-off or shed position.

Coaching Points: Emphasize high knee action when crossing over with the off leg. Stress quickness and speed. Work left and right.

5. Turn Around and Sprint Drill (Figure 2-3)

Purpose: To develop body balance, leg-arm action and agility.

Procedure: On command, the players start running in place, using a high-knee action, pumping the arms vigorously, and turning slowly clockwise or counterclockwise. After one or two body revolutions, the coach gives a second command, "GO!" and the players whip around and sprint 10 yards in the direction they faced initially.

Coaching Points: Warm-up players thoroughly before having them sprint. Stress coordinated high knee-arm action.

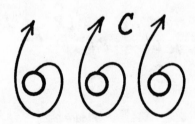

Figure 2-3

6. Spot Running or Footfire Drill

Purpose: To develop body balance, leg-arm action and agility.

Procedure: Same setup as (5) Turn Around and Sprint Drill, only on command players sprint in place as fast as they can, pounding their feet into the ground rapidly. Go five seconds footfire, five seconds rest, five seconds footfire, etc.

Coaching Points: Stress quickness and rapidity in moving the feet. Keep the feet close to the ground (about two inches) in order to touch the feet to the ground as rapidly as possible. Do not extend drill unless conditioning is desired, instead of agility and reaction.

7. Stationary High-Knee Running Drill

Purpose: To develop body balance, quickness, and high-knee running action.

Procedure: Same as for (6) Spot Running or Footfire Drill, only on command players lift knees high and pump legs rapidly sprinting in place, while alternately touching knees to palms of hands which are held waist high parallel to the ground. Sprint rapidly for five seconds, rest five seconds, sprint, rest, etc.

Coaching Points: Stress correct body alignment and good running form. Run on toes and balls of feet, not on heels. Lift knees to palms of hands, not lower palms to knees. If drill is used for conditioning—sprint, jog, sprint, jog, instead of resting between commands.

8. Forward High-Knee Running Drill

Purpose: To develop body balance, leg-arm action and high-knee running action.

Procedure: Same as for (6) Spot Running or Footfire Drill, only on command players lift knees high and pump legs rapidly using vigorous arm action while moving forward for 5 yards. The body assumes a slight forward lean, and the head is kept up at all times. The drill should also be done on the balls of the feet and toes.

Coaching Points: Stress high-knee action, good body alignment and correct running form. The emphasis is not on sprinting 5 yards, but on the vigorous running action, causing the body to move (creep) forward.

9. Forward-Backward-Sprint Drill (Figure 2-4)

Purpose: To develop body balance, leg-arm action, coordination and agility.

Procedure: On command, players run forward, using chopping steps and pumping arm action. On second, third, fourth, etc. commands, until they hear, "Sprint!," they whip themselves around 180° with force of shoulders and hips, and continue running backward, forward, etc. until final commands, then sprint 10 yards. Line of direction remains the same throughout the drill, always moving away from initial lineup position.

Coaching Points: Stress quickness, speed, good form and body alignment when running.

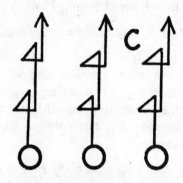

Figure 2-4

10. Running Backward Drill

Purpose: To develop body balance and leg action.

Procedure: Same as (9) Forward-Backward-Sprint Drill, only players line up facing away from the direction they intend to run backward. On command players run backward, with a slight body lean forward rather than backward, staying on the toes and balls of the feet.

Coaching Points: Emphasize quickness and speed. Emphasis is not on high-knee action as this forces the torso up and the head back.

11. Grab Grass or Scoop Drill

Purpose: To develop body balance and recovery, coordination, reaction and agility.

Procedure: May be organized the same as (1) High Stepper Drill where players follow each other across the width of the field at 5-yard intervals, over and back. On command, the first player sprints at top speed for 5 yards, bends over and tries to "scoop" or grab a handful of grass, regains his balance, sprints another 5 yards, bends to opposite side and grabs grass with his near hand, regains balance, alternating from right side to left side, across the field. When the first player bends to scoop, send the second player after the lead player, and continue at about 5-yard intervals until all players are in the drill. Repeat procedure coming back across from the opposite side of the field. Or the drill may be set up with players in three lines, using the length of the field. The first three players leave on command, and the coach continues to give commands each time he wants the players to bend and grab grass, for a specified distance.

Coaching Points: Drill is to simulate body balance and recovery after being tripped or partially tripped. Stress speed, quickness and reaction to commands.

12. Forward Rolls (somersault) Drill

Purpose: To develop body balance and agility, and to teach how to fall and roll correctly on the ground and to regain feet to an upright position.

Procedure: Players start from a low position, literally rolling into the drill rather than diving into it initially. The initial shock is taken by the hands as the palms are placed on the ground. The chin is tucked forward on the breastbone as the player buckles his body and brings his knees into his chest. As the elbows bend, cushioning the impact with the ground, the weight is caught on the shoulder blades at the base of the neck, and transferred downward to the buttocks as the player rolls. He grasps both ankles and gives an additional tuck and pull to create the necessary momentum to pull himself up onto his feet into a good football position. Repeat.

Coaching Points: Stress low center of gravity and proper method of landing on the ground.

13. Broadjumping-Somersault-Sprint Drill (Figure 2-5)

Purpose: To develop body balance and agility, and to teach how to land correctly on the ground from an upright position.

Procedure: Starting from a good football position, players broadjump with both feet together twice, somersault once, and come up running for 10 yards farther.

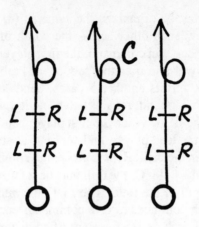

Figure 2-5

Coaching Points: Stress quickness, knee bend to get spring and leg snap when jumping, and low center of gravity and proper method of landing on the ground.

14. Broadjump-Somersault-Wave Drill

Purpose: To teach agility and reaction.

Procedure: Starting from a good football position, (see Drill 13), players broadjump with both feet together twice, somersault once, regain their feet quickly, and react to the coach's hand signal. If coach raises his hand above head, players, upon regaining feet, will sprint toward him, yell, "Pass!" and raise hands upward as they approach coach simulating throwing a pass. If coach makes a lateral movement with his hand, upon regaining feet, players will plant far foot and break at a 90° angle from their original direction using a crossover step on the correct angle of pursuit.

Coaching Points: Stress quickness, knee bend to get spring and leg snap when jumping, low center of gravity when somersaulting, and alertness for coach's hand signal. Avoid false-stepping or running in an arc when reacting to coach's lateral hand movement.

15. Somersault-Shed-Wave Drill (Figure 2-6)

Purpose: To teach agility, shedding or warding off an opponent and reaction.

Procedure: From a good football position execute a somersault, come to the feet in a good hitting position, with both hands executing forearm lifts, the defender warding off or shedding the blocker and then reacting to the coach's hand signal, taking the proper angle of pursuit.

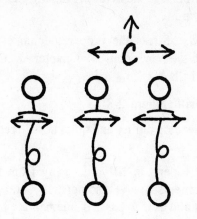

Figure 2-6

Coaching Points: Stress low center of gravity for defender as he executes his forward roll. Offensive man permits defender to regain his feet before stepping forward and executing shoulder lift or offensive block. Give hand signal quickly so defender can shed blocker and react immediately. Alternate shoulders and direction of pursuit. No false-stepping. Plant far foot and break at 90° angle, using crossover step.

16. Somersault and Tackle Drill (Figure 2-7)

Purpose: To teach agility, reaction and form-tackling.

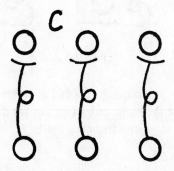

Figure 2-7

Procedure: From a good football position execute a somersault and come to the feet in a hitting position ready to form-tackle the ball carrier, who will step forward just as the defender regains his feet. Tackler carries ball carrier back 5 yards.

Coaching Points: Stress the proper mechanics of good tackling, which will be discussed in detail in Chapter 3. (See Chapter 3 for additional tackling drills.)

17. Mirror Drill (Figure 2-8)

Purpose: To develop agility and quickness in reacting and changing direction.

Procedure: "Leader" is 10 yards away from followers who will "mirror" his movements—wave, somersault, crab, grass drill, until "leader" raises his hand as if to pass. If linemen are performing the drill, they terminate the drill by yelling "Pass!" and sprint toward the leader, raising their hands upward as they approach him. If secondary defenders are performing the drill, they, too, sound off when the leader raises his hand simulating a pass, but drop off to cover their zones.

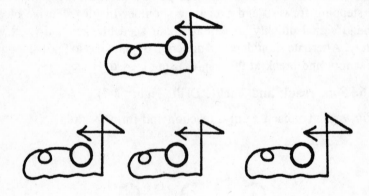

Figure 2-8

Coaching Points: Stress quickness and do not permit leader to extend reactions beyond five or drill will be ineffective for developing agility and reaction. It then becomes a conditioning drill.

18. Lateral Wave Drill

Purpose: To develop quickness, agility and reaction to movement.

Procedure: From a semiupright stance in a good football position, the players watch the coach's hand signals, responding quickly to the direction designated, always moving at right angles when changing directions, and using a crossover step when going laterally. If the players are linemen, the coach may conclude the drill by dropping a football to the ground simulating a fumble. Linemen must yell, "Ball!" and sprint either to recover the fumble or "scoop" up the ball, depending on whether or not rough work is desired and indicated by the coach. If backs are doing the drill, when coach raises ball overhead, defenders yell, "Pass!" and simulate dropping off to cover their zones.

Coaching Points: Stress quickness, no false-stepping, run at right angles instead of in an arc when changing direction, and no more than five reactions, or drill will become a conditioner instead of agility-reaction drill.

19. Crab or Scramble Drill (Figure 2-9)

Purpose: To develop quickness, agility and reaction to movement.

Procedure: Same as for (18) Lateral Wave Drill, but players are down in a four-point stance, tail low, head up, back straight, weight evenly distributed on fingertips and toes, reacting to hand signals of coach. Bring players up and running after fifth reaction.

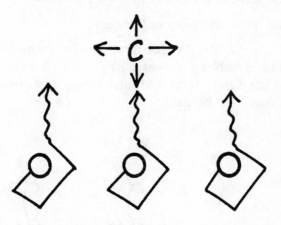

Figure 2-9

Coaching Points: Same as for (18) Lateral Wave Drill, only players use short, choppy steps, not crossing hands and feet when moving laterally, operating from a good balanced football position and moving quickly, simulating defensive moves or pursuit after being knocked down by a blocker or continuing to scramble after slipping off a block.

20. Shoulder Rolls Drill

Purpose: To develop body balance and agility and to teach how to land and roll on the ground correctly.

Procedure: As in (12) Forward Rolls Drill, the players start from a low position, literally rolling into the drill, rather than diving to the ground, in order to avoid injuries. The player should fling his left hand and forearm between his legs, turn his head to the opposite side so his chin is against his collarbone, buckle his left leg and push off with his right foot, as his body weight and momentum will carry him forward into his roll. The point of the shoulder is downward and inward when the same hand is extended to the rear between the legs, and the impact is taken on the back of the shoulder blade and transferred diagonally down across the body to the buttocks and feet, as the player completes his roll. He comes up into a good football position, flings the opposite hand and forearm (right) between his legs and rolls over the back of the right shoulder. Repeat.

Coaching Points: Stress flinging the arm and getting the point of the shoulder downward and inward. The roll is diagonally and not laterally. Stress proper method of landing and rolling.

21. Seat Rolls and Crab Drill (Figure 2-10)

Purpose: To teach agility and reaction.

Procedure: Player crabs, then flips his body over rolling on his seat, and then continues crabbing. Repeat drill right and left, somersault, regain feet, forearm lift man in front, and finally the player turns to meet the opponent coming from behind.

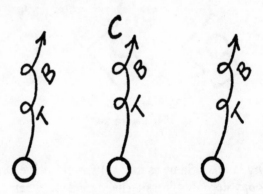

Figure 2-10

Coaching Points: Stress low center of gravity, quickness and operating from a good football position. Can use oral or hand signals for reactions.

22. Three-Man Log Roll Drill with Shed, Tackle, and Pursue Progressions (Figure 2-11)

Purpose: To develop agility and reaction in getting up off the ground; shedding a blocker; tackling; and shedding, pursuing and tackling.

Procedure: Players are on the ground on all fours, 5 yards apart. On coach's command No. 1 goes over No. 2, and the latter rolls to the outside. Then No. 3 goes over No. 1. The player from the outside goes over the player in the middle, and rolls to the opposite side. The player in the middle stays low and rolls to the outside. Drill is continuous until the coach yells, "Up!" If both lines are log rolling at the same time when command "Up" is given, offensive players try to block defenders, who will shed them; move forward and are form-tackled by the defensive men; and block defenders, who will shed them, pursue and tackle (tag) the ball carrier (coach) or react to coach's hand signals.

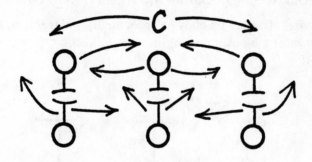

Figure 2-11

Coaching Points: Drills are done in a series of three-man units. Stress quickness.

23. Spinning Drill

Purpose: To develop body balance and coordination.

Procedure: A two-man "buddy" drill with any even number of players performing drill at the same time. First player gets on all fours on the ground. Second player rests his chest on the back of the player on all fours. His feet are spread so that he has room to operate in a semicircle from the head of the down player to either side, back to his hips. He may hold his hands and arms away from his body for balance, or place them behind his back. On the coach's commands of "Right," "Left," etc., he moves in the specified direction as quickly as possible. He should stay on his toes and the balls of his feet.

Coaching Points: Stress quickness. If top man is permitted to make a complete circle, caution must be used so that he does not step on the down man's ankles or trip over his extended feet.

24. Crab-Circle-Crab Drill

Purpose: To develop agility and reaction.

Procedure: From a four-point stance head up, tail down, back straight, good base, weight on the hands and balls of the feet, respond to hand and verbal signals of coach, including circling of right arm, circling left arm, and come up running.

Coaching Points: Do not extend for too many reactions or drill becomes a conditioner. Stress quickness, including circling.

25. Quarter-Eagle, Sprint-Wave Drill (Figure 2-12)

Purpose: To develop body balance, agility and reaction, simulating moving to meet a blocker coming from any direction.

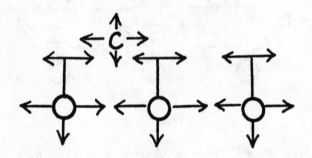

Figure 2-12

Procedure: Players in a semiupright stance with knees partly flexed, head up, tail down, hands and arms away from the body in a good defensive football position. On command or starting count, players start hopping in place, both feet together, similar to the rapidity of moving the feet in (6) Spot Running or Footfire Drill. On coach's commands of "Right!" "Right!" "Left!" "Left!" players execute one-quarter turns until coach yells "Sprint!" or "Go!" They whirl around, if facing away from the coach and their original position and sprint toward him. As they approach the coach, he indicates direction of lateral movement they are to take.

Coaching Points: Stress quickness when hopping in place and turning. Do not give too many quarter turns (reactions) or drill becomes a conditioner instead of agility-reaction drill.

26. Running Ropes or Rope Maze Drills

    I. Single-Stepping Rope Drills:
       a) Every one.
       b) Every other one.
    II. Two-Feet-Together Rope Drills:
       a) Every one and every other one.
       b) Forward and laterally.
    III. Carioca Rope Drills:
       a) Laterally.
       b) In the same line.

Purpose: To develop body balance, coordination and agility.

Procedure: The stationary ropes are 60 feet in length, 1 foot high, and 4 feet (two lanes) or 6 feet (three lanes) wide, so that each individual "box" is 2 feet wide and 1½ feet in length. Players are in single or double file, depending on whether or not one or both lanes are used for the specific drill. Drills are conducted just like (1) High Stepper and (2) Carioca.

Coaching Points: Same as Drills 1 and 2. Ropes may be used for a number of other drills, too, where applicable. Backs may carry a football and shift it from arm to arm.

Chapter 3

TACKLING FUNDAMENTALS
AND TECHNIQUES

TACKLING IS THE KEY TO GOOD DEFENSIVE FOOTBALL. A poor tackling team affects the morale and reduces the total effectiveness of its own offense by limiting its offensive scoring opportunities when it fails to force the opposition to give up the football to them. On the other hand, a good, hard-tackling defensive football team usually is difficult to defeat, and limits the number of times the opposition has the football. Nothing fires up the offense like a tough defense that turns the ball over to them on a big play. The best test of a team's morale is its tackling ability. Defensively, a team is no better than its tackling. The highest tribute a team can be paid is to be called a fine, hard-tackling, hard-hitting football team.

Coaches differ in their opinions concerning the best tackling techniques, but all agree the objective is to down the ball carrier and/or to prevent him from carrying out his specific assignment.

To execute all of the defensive fundamentals correctly during the actual tackle, and then failing to tackle or stop the ball carrier means total failure. All has been in vain if the defensive player fails to accomplish this objective, since tackling is the ultimate of defensive football.

Regardless of the techniques employed, effective tackling is the true test of defensive football. Gang tackles or team pursuit to the tackle is icing on the cake.

BASIC QUALITIES: DESIRE AND FORM

Tackling consists of two basic qualities, *desire* and *form*. Of the two, *desire* is the more important requisite and generally is considered to be at least 75 percent of effective tackles. If a player has the desire, generally he has the other inherent qualities of pride, morale and courage in order to tackle aggressively and effectively. Some players can allow themselves to be hit; a defensive player is an athlete who hits other people.

Tackling ability can be improved since *form* can be taught. A defensive man can usually bring down a ball carrier regardless of the form used if he has the determination and guts to get the job done. A player tackles better if he has the desire to punish the ball carrier.

PRINCIPLES AND FUNDAMENTALS OF TACKLING

The *good tackle* is the head-on tackle. It is the type of tackle that completely destroys the ball carrier. It leaves little doubt in his mind as to who is the master of the situation. Despite the wide scope in techniques allowed a tackler, the following are the cardinal principles and fundamentals of good tackling:

(1) The instant before contact as the tackler approaches the ball carrier, he should be in a "ready" or "hitting" position. This means having a good base, feet apart approximately shoulder-width and moving with short choppy steps being careful not to overstride, weight low in the butt, knees flexed in order to be able to uncoil and deliver a blow into the ball carrier. The back is relatively straight, head up, eyes on the stomach which is the tackler's target, arms and hands away from the body, feet apart for a good base, with body under control and on balance. From this good "hitting" position, the tackler is able to shift with the runner and his solid base gives him a good foundation for a driving tackle.

(2) The tackler must time his contact and drive his forehead through the football to get a good *shoulder* tackle. If the runner carries the football on either side of his body, the tackler's head will clear the ball carrier's body and he will get a solid shoulder tackle instead of an arm tackle. By directing his forehead rather than the top of his helmet at the football, the tackler can react better to the ball carrier since he is able to keep his eyes on the target. Very seldom does the good ball carrier run straight at an opponent, or try to run over him unless he has no other choice. Since the ball carrier is likely to fake one way and go another, the tackler must

maintain a good base and not lose his target by lowering his head. He must have his head up and eyes open in order to see his target. There is no way of having power unless the tackler's head is up.

Explode with the eyes through the ball with the top of the helmet in the ball carrier's armpit.

(3) As the tackler makes contact, he should extend his arms and hands and simultaneously "club" them around the ball carrier's body, and employ a wrist lock or grasp his hands prior to using his strong back and leg muscles to lift the ball carrier off the ground. He must explode his arms up through the hips of the runner, not swing them wide around the runner. He could lose a shoulder by throwing his arms around rather than up and through. He should hit, rap and lift by extending his body and legs, stopping the forward progress of the ball carrier, and take the latter's legs away from him. The power of the hit is based on how fast the tackler rotates his hips into the runner. Football is played with the legs. Many times a defensive man will make good shoulder contact, but fail to make the tackle. The ball carrier's feet maintain contact with the ground, he regains his balance and continues running because the tackler fails to get his arms around him and follow through. You must carry your legs all the way through the tackle, also.

"Clubbing" the arms does not mean swinging them open wide laterally, since the exaggerated arm swing usually causes the tackler to drop his head and stop.

(4) The follow-through consists of hitting on the rise up into the ball carrier's numbers, picking him up and slamming him to the ground on his back or side with the tackler on top of him. The ball carrier should never be permitted to fall forward.

Tackling relies heavily upon the application of the principle of power and leverage. Despite minor differences of opinion in the various techniques, good tackling is based upon these previously mentioned fundamentals.

Despite the fact coaches refer to tackling as shoulder, angle (side), open field, from-the-rear, the high-sideline, tackling-the-passer, and gang tackling—the first two actually cover all classifications of tackling. Excluding tackling from the rear, if a tackle is not a shoulder then it must be at an angle, whether it is near the line of scrimmage, in the open field, on the sideline or tackling the passer. Gang tackling, of course, is both angle and head-on as all of the defensive players hustle to tackle the ball carrier before the whistle stops the play or the runner is downed.

The shoulder tackle generally is used in those situations in which the ball carrier has limited space in which to maneuver, and usually occurs at or near the line of scrimmage or in some cases in the close secondary. The tackler meets the ball carrier.

Most of the tackles made in football are actually angle tackles, as seldom does a tackler meet the ball carrier head-on and execute a "picture" tackle. The fundamentals of the angle tackle are similar with two additions; the first coaching point being that the tackler places his head across and in front of the ball carrier. The objective is twofold: (1) it increases his tackling surface and gives additional power for the tackle; and (2) in the event the tackler is not successful in making the tackle but gets his head across and in front of the ball carrier, it forces the latter into pursuing tacklers. The objective is to keep the latter into pursuing tacklers; to keep containment on the ball carrier, turn him to the inside and keep him in front of the defenders. This will be discussed in greater detail shortly when considering team pursuit and gang tackling. Should the would-be tackler fail to turn the ball carrier to the inside, say as the result of incorrectly driving his head behind the runner, and he gets outside of containment, then the defenders become "chasers" instead of pursuers and it is merely a foot race between them and the ball carrier.

The tackler must also get his front leg and hip in front of the runner. At the moment of impact, the second point occurs. He must pivot the front foot into the runner and explode through his front hip and up through the runner. Two things happen: first the runner, even if much bigger than the tackler, will still fall over him not run through him; secondly, it puts the tackler in the best possible position to put the runner on his back. A good rap is still mandatory.

The approach for tackling the passer is more reckless and higher. The tackler should keep his eyes on the passer's eyes and arm, as the latter will tell the tackler what he is going to do. As the tackler approaches the passer and is within a couple of yards of him, he should raise his hands as high as possible with the idea of tackling the football, forcing the passer to fumble if possible. The tackler should follow through with arms crashing down hard on the passer, pinning his passing arm to his side. This will stop the passer from making a desperate pass, or from legally grounding the ball. Many good passers complete passes with tacklers around their legs.

Assuming he gets beyond the line of scrimmage and is approaching the safety man or one of the defensive halfbacks, a good ball carrier has an advantage over the defender. The latter has too much territory to protect, and in such a situation the defender is not necessarily trying to save yards, but is trying to prevent a touchdown. Therefore, the defender must make the ball carrier commit himself to one side or the other, limiting his running room and the territory the defensive man must defend. When the ball carrier is in open field, he should be maneuvered to such a position that the tackler can run him out-of-bounds if he continues in the same line. If he cuts back, he will run into the arms of the pursuit. This is a "sure" tackle, but it is not a "pretty" one as the ball carrier must be tackled high (or pushed aggressively out-of-bounds).

If the ball carrier cannot be maneuvered into the sideline, the tackler must maneuver and retreat as he defends his goal line, until he can get help from his pursuing teammates. If the tackler must take his "shot" at the ball carrier, he must still force him to go only one way. When they are even with each other, then the tackler must go after the ball carrier aggressively, remembering to drive his head in front of the ball carrier getting in between the runner and the goal line. This is an angle tackle with the concept being not to drive the runner to his back, but just to get a piece of him and hang on.

The same principles of tackling a player from the rear prevail as in the other types of tackles. Assuming a pursuing defender is overtaking a slower running ball carrier, then contact should be made about waist high with the arms sliding downward to grasp the ball carrier's legs dragging him to the ground. The tackler should aim high and be fairly close to the ball carrier before he dives for him so that the latter's forward progress or his last-second evasive tactic does not carry him out of the tackler's range and grasp. The tackler should not leap on the ball carrier's back, as the latter is likely to carry him for extra yardage downfield.

Assuming the ball carrier is fast and is running away from the pursuer, any effort to tackle him generally is in desperation. One technique the tackler can use is to dive at the heels of the ball carrier, attempting to trip him by slapping the one (rear) foot hard toward his opposite foot. When the pursuer is successful, frequently this causes the ball carrier to trip and fall.

The importance and necessity of the proper angles of team pursuit and gang tackling cannot be stressed enough.

There is a difference between gang tackling and piling on the ball carrier. Cheap shots have no place in the game. When we watch films, we look for three players to be in on each tackle, and when we stop the picture (still action) the moment the runner hits the ground, we want to see nine of our people in the picture!

Team Pursuit Defined

It is generally believed that the most important factor in defensive football today is the proper angle of team pursuit. Many coaches consider this as the starting point for a discussion on defensive football. Team pursuit may be defined as a planned system of converging upon the man who has the football as quickly as possible, with the intent of the entire defensive team taking the proper angles and arriving at the ball together. Containing the ball carrier inside of the defensive perimeter requires that you maintain proper pursuit angles in order to obtain gang tackling.

Gang tackling is the most demoralizing tactic in football against your opponent, and is a *must* for good defensive play. Therefore, every defender should hustle to tackle the ball carrier on every play. Never give up!

There have been many changes made in the game of football over the years. However, a team which displays desire, hustle and enthusiasm, and one on which each player works hard to improve his quickness, speed and tackling until he is doing his very best, will produce a squad that will win more than it will lose.

TACKLING DRILLS

In drilling, a coach should strive to teach his players the proper form in tackling, without destroying their desire and determination.

1. Form Tackling Drill (Figure 3-1)

Purpose: To teach and develop the fundamentals and techniques of tackling.

Procedure: Ball carrier lines up inside a 5-yard square approximately 3 yards from the front line. Opposite and facing him 1 yard away from the front line, outside of the square, is the tackler in a "ready" position, feet digging, eyes focused on the target (offensive man's numerals if football is not used in drill). On coach's command, the ball carrier moves into the tackler at about half-speed. Just before contact, the tackler takes one step forward, dips his knees and makes contact with his forehead. The tackler places his forehead on the numerals and slides it to one side or the other for a shoulder tackle. Tackler wraps arms around opponent's buttocks, squeezes him up, and carries him backward for 5 yards to the far end of the square.

This is a walk-through drill—form is the most important factor. The runner should also hop up in the air at impact to help the tackler work on form. End-result drill—we often use this drill very early in the practice year. The tackler is walked into the final position of impact, he then is taken backward out of the position. This type of walk-through helps the player visualize the exact position he should be in.

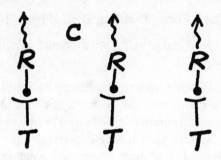

Figure 3-1

Coaching Points: Stress proper fundamentals and which technique should be used in tackling. If football is used, tackler drives forehead into the football (target) in order to eliminate closing his eyes, dropping and turning his head, and tackling. Stress acceleration of the feet at contact (leg lift) to get maximum power. Ball carrier should not jump upward assisting the tackler. Latter should hit and lift, and drive through his opponent, not merely to him.

2. Butt Ball Tackling Drill (Figure 3-2)

Purpose: To develop the fundamentals and techniques of tackling, quickness and body control.

Procedure: Ball carrier runs back and forth laterally within a 5-yard square remaining parallel to the front line, switching the football to the side toward which he is moving. From a position opposite the ball carrier and staying parallel with him, the tackler butts the football with his forehead, recovers, butts, recovers, trying to knock the ball out of the ball carrier's arm. Upon coach's command, he tackles the ball carrier, employing the techniques described in detail previously.

Figure 3-2

Coaching Points: Stress quickness, movement, good football position and fundamentals of tackling.

3. Back-to-Back Form Tackling Drill (Figure 3-3)

Purpose: To teach and develop the fundamentals and techniques of tackling.

Procedure: Ball carrier and tackler line up back-to-back facing away from each other. On first command, both players walk slowly away from each other. On the second command, both whirl and turn, with ball carrier moving on a predetermined path at a right or left oblique angle or coming straight at the tackler. Latter must sprint and meet ball carrier at the "crossroads," executing the proper form as in Drills 1 and 2. If head-on, he carries ball carrier back 5 yards before setting him down on his feet. Speed up drill, going "live" after several turns left, right and head-on.

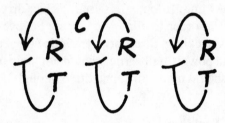

Figure 3-3

Coaching Points: Stress proper fundamentals and techniques of good tackling. When going live, give second command quickly so players do not get too far apart before tackling. Conclude drill live with ball carrier free-lancing, i.e., taking any course he wants to after the second command to evade the tackler.

4. Angle Tackling Drill (Figure 3-4)

Purpose: To teach the proper position and execution of the method most often used in a game.

Procedure: Two lines of athletes 5 yards apart and facing the coach who is 8 yards in front of tackler group so that the group to be tackled must run at an angle to him. This is a ¾-speed drill. On command, the tackler gets in an eagle position (hitting position) facing the other group. On second command, the the runner moves at an angle toward coach, the tackler moves across and meets him with the proper form—head in front and across the bow; front leg in front of runner with hips down. Throw the clubs (forearms) up and through the hips, rotate the front leg and hip, then explode up into the runner. Pick him up and carry him 3 steps and set him down. We can also do this into a pit for complete effect. But, we don't take the man to the ground.

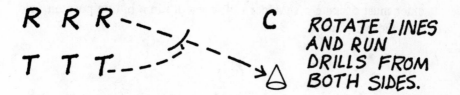

Figure 3-4

Coaching Points: Make sure tackler has feet apart, hips down, head in front, leg in front, good rotation into the runner (rotate the hips, not face, so that the tackler does not end up facing the runner). Throw the clubs and grasp the wrist, good extension and lift into the runner.

5. Supine Tackling Drill

Purpose: To teach and develop second reaction of getting up off the ground and executing the proper technique and fundamentals of tackling.

Procedure: Tackler in supine position on his back with the top of his helmet touching the front line of a 5-yard square. The football is placed 5 yards away at the back line of the square, at the heels of the ball carrier, who is facing away from the tackler. On the coach's command, the ball carrier must whirl around, pick up the football, attempt to evade the tackler, and get to the opposite side of the square. The tackler in turn must roll over quickly on the same command, spring to his feet, get in a good hitting position and tackle the ball carrier. Upright dummies are stationed 3 yards apart so the ball carrier has a limited area in which to evade the tackler.

Coaching Points: Stress proper fundamentals of tackling. If tackler is slow-footed in getting up from the ground, control the drill by giving him the command, but hold the football instead of putting it on the ground for the ball carrier to pick up. Then flip the ball to the ball carrier, who must whirl around and attempt to evade the tackler.

6. Shoulder Roll Tackling Drill (Figure 3-5)

Purpose: To teach and develop second reaction of getting up off the ground and executing the proper techniques and fundamentals of tackling.

Procedure: Same as (5) Supine Tackling Drill, but tackler is in an upright position facing the back of the ball carrier on the opposite side of the square and is several yards away from the front line. On the coach's command, the ball carrier whirls and does the same as previously. The tackler must execute a shoulder roll, come up in a hitting position, and tackle the ball carrier.

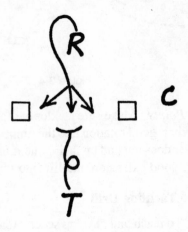

Figure 3-5

Coaching Points: Stress quickness, low center of gravity, proper shoulder roll, and proper fundamentals of tackling. Coach can control the drill to favor tackler, as in previous drill, by permitting tackler to regain feet before he tosses the football to the ball carrier.

7. Somersault Tackling Drill (Figure 3-6)

Purpose: To develop second reaction, quickness and the proper fundamentals of tackling.

Procedure: Tackler is opposite a 5-yard square, 2 yards back from the front line. To his left and right, and directly opposite, are ball carriers. On the coach's command, the tackler executes a somersault (forward roll or shoulder roll), and regains his feet, coming up in a good hitting position. Coach calls name of ball carrier, who sprints to opposite side of the square, trying to evade tackler.

Coaching Points: Stress proper fundamentals of tackling. Permit tackler to regain his feet before indicating which ball carrier is to cross the square.

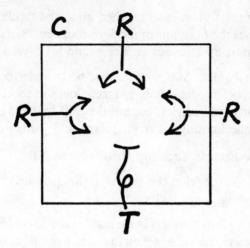

Figure 3-6

8. Wave-Shed-Tackle Drill (Figure 3-7)

Purpose: To develop agility, reaction and the proper fundamentals and techniques of tackling.

Procedure: Ball carrier and tackler are 10 yards apart, with a blocker half-way between them. Coach faces the blocker and the ball carrier, standing behind the tackler. Blocker moves back and forth laterally to the sides of his 5-yard square, and tackler must stay even and opposite him. After several movements laterally, by hard signal or oral command, blocker charges tackler but ball carrier cannot break until blocker gets to

Figure 3-7

tackler. Latter must meet blocker, shed him, and tackle the ball carrier before he crosses the front line of the 5-yard square. Ball carrier is limited laterally and must try to evade tackler within his 5-yard square.

Coaching Points: Stress quickness, body under control, shedding blocker and proper fundamentals and techniques of tackling. If tackler is too slow to catch ball carrier, control the drill by telling the ball carrier when to run, and limiting his running lane to 3 yards in width.

9. Circle-Escape Tackling Drill (Figure 3-8)

Purpose: To develop the proper techniques and fundamentals of tackling, including gang tackling.

Procedure: Ball carrier is in the middle of a 12-to-15-foot (diameter) circle. Rim men are tacklers, set up in a ready position, with feet moving and eyes on target. Ball carrier either tries to run between two defenders, or directly at a defender, in order to "escape" from the circle. If he attempts to go between, the men on each side of the gap must close it and both tackle the ball carrier. If he runs directly at a tackler, the latter must meet him head-on, and the tacklers on each side must close in for a gang tackle. Player who lets ball carrier "escape" replaces him in the middle of the circle.

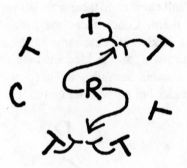

Figure 3-8

Coaching Points: Drill is "rough" so leave ball carrier in middle only three times if he does not "escape" sooner. Stress good tackling fundamentals and techniques.

10. 1-Versus-1 Tackling Drill

Purpose: To develop the proper techniques and fundamentals of open full tackling.

Procedure: Ball carrier and tackler are 5 yards apart, facing each other, with an upright dummy directly between them and a dummy 3 yards to either side so that the ball carrier must break off of the middle dummy and into the hole formed by it and one of the outside dummies. Coach flips ball to ball carrier and at the same time the tackler moves forward and sets up in a good football position, with feet moving, attempting to meet the ball carrier in the hole as he veers left or right off of the middle dummy.

Open-Field Tackling DB's

We use a variation of this drill for defensive backs. The 2 players are 10 yards apart in a 5-yard wide tunnel. On command, the runner starts forward and the DB back-pedals. At 5 yards the DB then changes direction as if he were on pass responsibility and suddenly reads run. He then moves forward and gets in good position for an open-field tackle. He can make one fake, and one only. The runner cannot try to run straight over tackler. We are working on tackling not looking for runners or useless injuries.

Coaching Points: Stress proper fundamentals and techniques of tackling. After flipping the ball to the ball carrier, attempt to watch the tackler's eyes. Getting into the proper position is the most important part of tackling, regardless of the player's size.

11. Open-Field Tackling Drill No. 1 (Figure 3-9)

Purpose: To teach defensive secondary men to ward off or shed a blocker, control him, and make the tackle in open field.

Procedure: Defensive secondary men set up in their positions from line of scrimmage. Blocker goes for one man, with ball carrier approxi-

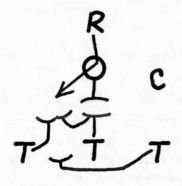

Figure 3-9

mately 3 yards behind him. Defender attempts to ward off blocker, control him, keep his feet free of the roll-back block, dispose of the blocker and tackle the ball carrier. Other two defenders close in on ball carrier and tackle him. Ball carrier can use any tactic to evade tacklers.

Coaching Points: Check pursuit angles of each defender. Stress open-field tackling techniques.

12. Open-Field Tackling Drill No. 2 (Figure 3-10)

Purpose: To develop reaction, pursuit and tackling in the open field.

Procedure: Defenders (linebackers or defensive secondary men) line up in a "ready" position on their 15-yard line, with the ball carrier on the 20-yard line. Lateral distance may be increased until defenders are attempting to protect width of field. Defenders move laterally with ball carrier, but do not pursue him until he crosses the 20-yard line and attempts to score. Defenders must take proper pursuit angles.

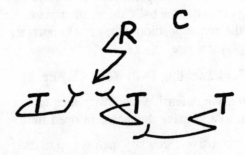

Figure 3-10

Coaching Points: Stress proper pursuit and open-field tackling fundamentals.

13. Sideline Tackling Drills: Tackler Versus Ball Carrier (Figure 3-11)

Purpose: To teach defensive backs to employ the sideline as the "12th man" on their team, and to make the sideline tackle.

Procedure: Ball carrier has a 6-yard running lane in which he may use any evasive tactic he wishes to get by the tackler (secondary defender). Tackler approaches ball carrier from inside-out and either tackles him high or aggressively pushes him out-of-bounds. When blocker is added, the defender must control the blocker, keep his feet free of a roll-block, dispose of the blocker, and force the ball carrier out-of-bounds. He should attempt to force the blocker into the ball carrier from inside out, narrowing the ball carrier's running lane.

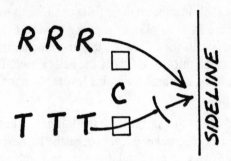

Figure 3-11

Coaching Points: Stress proper fundamentals and techniques of sideline tackling, and warding off a blocker.

14. Head Hunter Tackling Drill (Figure 3-12)

Purpose: To teach maintaining proper leverage (linebacker) on the ball carrier and to obtain practice in tackling.

Procedure: Upright dummies are placed on a straight line, allowing 5 feet between each dummy. Linebacker is in a ''ready'' position at one end of the dummies, across from the ball carrier. The coach flips the football to the ball carrier who either runs directly between two dummies, or fakes once and then goes into the next hole. The linebacker makes the tackle in the hole from an inside-out position, head across in front of the ball carrier.

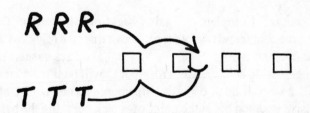

Figure 3-12

Coaching Points: Stress proper leverage and tackling fundamentals.

15. Machine Gun Tackling Drill

Purpose: To develop shedding a blocker, pursuit and tackling, especially for defensive ends and linebackers.

Procedure: Drill is either half or full speed, with the blockers or the coach regulating the flow of players moving toward the defender from a vertical, horizontal or diagonal line. As the first blocker makes contact, the second leaves, then the third, and finally the ball carrier. The defender hits, shuffles, hits, shuffles, hits and maintains leverage on the ball carrier as he moves to tackle him.

Coaching Points: Stress hitting, shedding blockers (not wrestling with blockers) and moving to keep leverage on the ball carrier. Blockers are in a vertical line. Stress proper fundamentals and techniques of tackling.

16. 3-on-3 Challenge Drill (defensively) (Figure 3-13)

Purpose: To teach defensive fundamentals and techniques, including defeating the 1-on-1 block, controlling blocker, locating the football, pursuing and (gang) tackling the ball carrier.

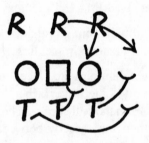

Figure 3-13

Procedure: Complete offensive backfield in straight T formation, plus offensive center and two other offensive linemen (tackles) versus three defensive linemen 1-on-1 (3-on-3), "live." The back receiving the hand-off (counter, inside belly, drive, cross-buck) will be live and the other two backs will fake. All three offensive linemen execute 1-on-1 blocks, with the defensive linemen not at the point-of-attack pursuing the ball carrier for gang tackling. Inside dummies are removed and ball carrier tries to evade three defensive linemen.

Coaching Points: Since drill is an "All Purpose Drill" which may be used either offensively or defensively, here use it for teaching pursuit and tackling. Do not use better running backs as ball carrier since three defenders are likely to tackle him. Stress all defensive fundamentals and techniques.

17. Bag Tackling Drill (Figure 3-14)

Purpose: To teach pursuit, reaction and tackling.

Procedure: Two upright dummies are 5 yards apart, with the coach in between them but several yards away. One at a time, but in rapid succession, tackler sprints from the coach's left (or right), squares off facing him, and then reacts to the coach's hand signal. Latter holds tackler in position momentarily, then quickly points to one of the upright dummies to his right or left. Tackler watches coach, pumps his feet, then sprints and tackles bag indicated by the coach. Managers man the bags. In the meantime, the next tackler has already sprinted to a position opposite the coach, awaiting his hand signal.

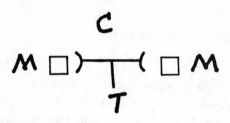

Figure 3-14

Coaching Points: Coach may shuffle and head fake, etc., and defender will position him, setting up in a hitting position, until coach indicates which bag should be tackled. Stress the proper fundamentals and techniques of tackling. Work right, left, diagonally with head-up coming toward the coach.

18. Tipper-Tackler Drill (Figure 3-15)

Purpose: To react to the ball that is tipped and intercepted, and to tackle the interceptor.

Procedure: "Tipper" turns and tackles the "trailer" who intercepts the ball. Tipper (tackler) runs forward and deflects the pass, thrown by the passer (coach), backward toward the trailer.

Coaching Points: Stress either tackling (this drill), or catching the deflected pass (Tip Interception Drill). If the former, then "tipper" turns and tackles the "trailer" regardless of whether or not he catches the deflected ball. If using drill for teaching catching a deflected ball, do not permit tipper to tackle trailer.

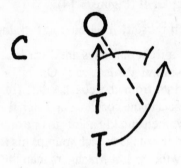

Figure 3-15

19. 2-Man Sled Tackling Drills

Purpose: To teach and develop the fundamentals of tackling.

Procedure: Sled is allowed to run free and is not scotched or weighted for single tackler. When working in pairs, sled is weighted with one man. For closeup tackling, player(s) in defensive stance. On coach's movement, simulating offensive center snapping the ball, tackler(s) hits, lifts, follows through, stops on whistle.

Coaching Points: Stress fundamentals of proper tackling, including proper approach, shock and impact with lift, follow through with good second effort.

20. Sled-Bags Tackling Drill (Figure 3-16)

Purpose: To teach defensive line fundamentals, including pursuit and tackling.

Procedure: Sled is scotched and is not permitted to run free. Coach on sled rattles it, simulating offensive movement or ball has been snapped. Defensive linemen covering pads on 2-man Crowther sled deliver a blow (flipper) and come to balance. Coach indicates direction of ball carrier (simulated) right or left. Defenders must react by jumping over dummies which have been placed on the ground parallel to and outside the arms of the sled, and tackle upright dummies which are approximately 5 to 8 yards to the rear of the defenders' initial positions.

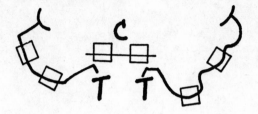

Figure 3-16

Coaching Points: Tacklers should each tackle a bag and roll it over. Stress proper fundamentals of pursuit and tackling, after delivering a blow and coming to balance. Drill should be done rapidly, but correctly. Managers should set up bags quickly in order to keep the drill moving rapidly.

Chapter 4

DEFENSIVE LINE FUNDAMENTALS AND TECHNIQUES

DEFENSIVE FOOTBALL IS REACTION FOOTBALL

Defensive play is reaction football because the defenders must react after the ball has been snapped. Mistakes by the offense generally mean loss of yardage, loss of the down, and perhaps loss of the football. Mistakes on the part of only one man on the defensive team to react properly may result in a touchdown for the offense. This pertinent factor cannot be minimized, and must be stressed frequently, if the objectives of defensive football are to be realized.

Regardless of the defensive alignment, the principles of defensive line play are breakdown block protection, fight through resistance, read play action, pursuit and tackling. The basic defensive fundamentals which must be taught to all linemen are as follows:

1. Stance: three- or four-point stance.
2. Alignments: head-on, eye, shoulder, cocked and offset or flexed.
3. Charges: control the opponent, control one side of him or the other, penetrate, gap-charge, loop, slant, stunts.

4. Responsibilities: own gap, angle of pursuit, leverage on ball, pass rush, lane reaction to reads, and reaction to traps, double-teams, sweep and linemen.
5. Tackling: head-on, angle (side), and gang tackling.

Move on Movement or on the Snap of the Ball

From a good defensive stance, the lineman must be able to charge quickly, moving on the movement of the offensive lineman opposite him or on the movement of the football. At the same time he must be able to protect himself against the opponent directly opposite him on a straight charge, and still key offensive linemen to attack side. Should either lineman attack him, the defender must react quickly, still maintaining good balance and direct his charge at the lineman. Should neither attack him, the defender should continue with his original charge, destroying his opponent's block. In either case, the defender must retain his block breakdown and pad distance so that he has freedom of movement and can react properly.

Lineman's defensive stance. Excluding the stance of the defensive ends, who may or may not be in a semiupright two-point stance depending upon their duties and responsibilities in a particular defensive front, the interior linemen will employ a three- or four-point stance. The weight will be evenly distributed on feet and hand(s), since the defender must be able to step with either foot first. His center of gravity is likely to be lower than when in his offensive stance, since a defensive lineman's base will be wider as his feet are wider than his shoulders. His feet will be staggered more so than in an offensive stance, although his rear foot cannot extend much farther than beyond the heel of his forward foot or the defensive lineman will have difficulty stepping quickly with either foot, especially if slanting, veering or looping. His down hand, if he employs a three-point stance, will correspond to his rear foot, although some coaches specify a left- or right-handed stance for the defensive linemen on the right and left side of the line, respectively, as they prefer having the outside foot forward. Other coaches prefer a "natural" stance, and the defensive linemen are permitted to stagger either foot.

The weight on the down hand depends on whether the defensive lineman always charges straight forward or varies his charge, looping, slanting, or stunting. While he should not noticeably vary the amount of weight on his hand, tipping off the type of charge he is going to employ, with the exception of when he will take a gap charge and wants penetration, if he has too much weight forward he will encounter difficulty when stunting. He must be able to move quickly on the movement of the blocker opposite him or on the snap of the ball, or the blocker will outcharge him.

Some players are able to view both the movement of the ball and the opposition across the line of scrimmage simultaneously. These players should watch their opponent, move when the ball moves, and still be able to react to the movements of the opponent. There is a difference of opinion among coaches as to whether a defensive player should watch his opponent or the ball, and move on his opponent's movement or the snap of the ball. Under some conditions, coaches maintain the defender should watch only for the movement of his offensive opponent, while others stress watching the ball. This is especially true in the latter case where the defensive linemen are looping, slanting, stunting, etc., and not playing a straight hit-and-reaction type of defensive play.

Football is a game of contact, especially down in the pits. With emphasis on the reading-reacting type of defensive play, the inexperienced player in particular is likely to forget the necessity of first delivering a blow to his opponent, then reacting, in order to neutralize his charge, control him, and maintain freedom in order to carry out the other principles and fundamentals of defensive line play. The type of blow he delivers or his block breakdown techniques depend on the defensive philosophy of the coach. The most common types of block protection are the forearm or hand shiver and the forearm or shoulder lift.

(Forearm) or hand shiver techniques. The forearm shiver consists of stepping with the rear foot and hitting with the heels of the hands simultaneously under the shoulders of the opponent, in order to straighten him up, break and neutralize his charge. The feet should be even when the hands are extended forward. The wrists and elbows must be locked in order to deliver the blow with strength and authority. Otherwise the offensive player's charge will collapse the arms of the defender, and he can get at his legs with a shoulder block. The blow must be delivered from up under the blocker, and the defensive lineman must follow through with short driving steps until the ball is located or until he determines from where pressure is being exerted. He should then use his hands to throw the blocker away from him and start pursuit action.

(Forearm) or shoulder lift techniques. The shoulder and forearm should be coordinated with the same foot, which will give the strongest possible position. The defensive lineman takes a short step forward with either foot, and uncoils with the same shoulder and forearm, delivering a blow to the chest of the blocker, striking under his numerals with his forearm. The opposite hand is used for leverage on the blocker, keeping him away from the defender and destroying his balance.

The shoulder or forearm lift is generally used in a short-yardage situation, especially when the defense wants to meet force with force, as when near the goal line. This defensive maneuver should be executed from as low a position as possible. The defender must retain balance quickly, and be able to pursue laterally if the play is away from his area.

The charge of the defensive lineman must be low and hard, and each player must be on balance and in a good football position to move laterally if necessary. The defender must neutralize the offensive charge of the blocker so that he will control his assigned territory. The offensive team cannot make any yardage through any area of the line if every defensive lineman plays his position properly, and is not beaten by his offensive blocker. Second, by striking blows to the offensive linemen the whole way down the line, the off-side blockers cannot get in front of the ball carrier, aligning themselves with the running lane in order to lead interference or block downfield in the secondary.

In order for a defense to be successful, each player must reach his designated area on his charge. The areas of responsibility will differ depending upon each player's individual alignment, and his area of responsibility. He may be head-on, shade one side or the other of the opponent offsetting to various degrees and including either gap, or off the line of scrimmage. His alignment to his opponent may be nose-on-nose, nose-to-ear, foot-to-crotch, foot-to-foot or in the gap. His defensive charge may be to control the opponent opposite, control one side or the other, penetrate the gap, loop, slant or stunt into the offensive lineman or area to either side of the blocker opposite his initial alignment. His reaction after his charge, depending upon whether the ball is coming to or going away from him, should be to read play action and proper angle of pursuit.

Each player should be made to feel that his particular territory or area of responsibility is the most important area in the team's coordinated defense. Since the combination of all defenses becomes the coordinated team defense, it is necessary for each player to protect his position. Players know they will be blocked at times, but the good player does not stay blocked. He reacts and still protects his territory. The key is to get everyone to do his job and not worry about someone else's.

Each defender must locate the football or the ball carrier quickly before reacting. If the defender will fight pressure and fight through resistance, instead of looking into the backfield and watching the action there, he will not be fooled by the faking techniques. He must move first, deliver a blow, then locate the football before reacting. A common error for the inexperienced player is to attempt to locate the football without first delivering a blow. He takes the fake, and leaves his territory unprotected. The defensive lineman's key is in the immediate area of the blocker opposite him and those offensive linemen to either side. Although he may be fooled by influence blocking at times, if he reacts to his key and locates the ball carrier or the football, his defensive play will be sound.

Most coaches advocate that a defensive lineman should not run around a blocker. They feel that when this occurs the defender becomes a chase man instead of a pursuer, and he has blocked himself. Second, he will also open a running lane for the ball carrier. There are several ways of getting through a blocker to the ball carrier after contact is made. If the defender is more powerful than the blocker, he merely overpowers him and goes through the blocker. He can submarine through his man and plug a hole, or he can go over the blocker and attempt to make the tackle. Or he neutralizes the blocker, controls him, then breaks laterally in the direction of the ball carrier as the latter attempts to break off his blocker.

The importance and necessity of the proper angle of pursuit and gang tackling cannot be stressed too much. Team defense is the key to victory. Offenses can be run by stars. Defense must be a complete team effort on every play.

DEFENSIVE LINE DRILLS

1. Stance and Alignment Drill

Purpose: To teach the defender to line up properly, taking the correct lateral and vertical alignment in a good defensive football stance.

Procedure: Players pair off 1-versus-1, and defender assumes proper stance in relation to the offensive blocker, head-up or nose-on-nose; nose-to-ear, shoe-to-crotch, or shoe-to-shoe; offsetting both to the outside and inside, depending on the individual player's defensive position.

Coaching Points: Stress proper alignment and then stance, indicating whether defender's inside or outside foot should split the crotch of the blocker, or be inside, even with, or outside of the blocker's inside or outside foot. Stress importance of correct lateral and vertical alignment, depending upon the deployment of the defensive personnel, offensive splits and the tactical situation.

2. Block Breakdown Drills (Figure 4-1)

Purpose: To teach and develop defensive charge and block protection.

Procedure: Defender lines up in proper stance, depending upon which side of the defensive line he plays. Coach indicates defensive alignment, charge, and type of block protection to be employed. No starting count is employed as defender must react to first movement of blocker. After delivering his blow and destroying the block, he must be in a good football position ready to react to the coach's hand signal.

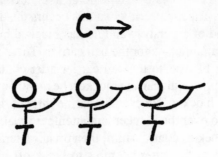

Figure 4-1

Coaching Points: Drill is controlled as emphasis is to move on movement (reason for not employing a starting count), deliver a blow (hand shiver or forearm lift), and be in a good football position ready to react, i.e., control blocker, locate the football, pursue and tackle.

3. Forearm or Shoulder Lift Drill

Purpose: To teach and develop using the forearm lift as block protection.

Procedure: Offensive player is on one (right) knee, back erect, head turned to the left, with the point of the chin on the left shoulder, right side of the body exposed. Coach stands behind offensive player, facing defender. Coach makes a quick hand movement, indicating snap of ball, and defender uncoils, coordinating (right) foot and flipper club, striking the exposed shoulder of the blocker, attempting to bowl him over.

Coaching Points: Hand dummies or air bags may be held by the blocker, and the defender may boom there. Stress when forearm or shoulder lift is employed. Stress bringing up feet, maintaining balance, and second reaction. Left and right, coordinating proper foot and forearm lift.

4. Reaction Drill

Purpose: To teach and develop the defensive principles of moving on movement (or the snap of the ball), deliver a blow, control blocker, locate the football, pursue and tackle the ball carrier.

Procedure: Coach stands behind defender, facing blocker and ball carrier. Latter two are flashed starting count, type of block, and direction ball carrier will run. Defender is given alignment, down and distance. On coach's starting count, blocker attempts to whip defender and vice versa. Latter must execute defensive fundamentals properly, pursue and tag the manager or tackle the ball carrier, if live.

Coaching Points: Stress proper alignment and stance initially. Stress throwing off blocker properly and not wrestling with him. Stress execution of proper defensive fundamentals and techniques.

5-6. 2-Man Sled Drills

5. *Forearm Lift and Reaction Drill* (Figure 4-2)

6. *Hand or Forearm Shiver and Reaction Drill*

(Same setup as Drill 5)

Purpose: To teach and develop block protection by using forearm lift (5) and hand shiver (6), and reaction to the ball.

Procedure: Defender lines up in defensive stance opposite arm or pad (5) or T-bar of sled (6). Coach stands on sled, and shakes it slightly simulating snap of ball. Defender executes forearm lift (5) or hand shiver (6), comes to balance, and then reacts to hand signal of coach indicating left, right or pass rush.

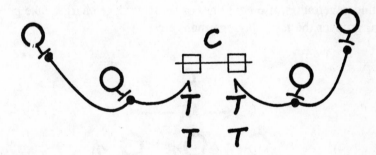

Figure 4-2

Coaching Points: For hand shiver, stress locking elbows and wrists and following through with short choppy steps until direction of pursuit is indicated. The heels of the hands are driven forward and upward (under the blocker's shoulder pads in an effort to straighten him up and neutralize his charge). Bring back foot up first. In forearm lift or boom, coordinate forearm-shoulder-foot, then come to balance quickly, watching coach for direction of pursuit. This drill can be effectively done on a 7-man sled also. You simply have the defender move down the sled reacting to each bag or every other bag. This can be achieved from a stance by firing out and sliding down, rolling, or spinning down to next bag.

7. Explosion or 1-Versus-2 Drills (progressive) (Figure 4-3)

Purpose: To teach delivering an explosive blow, gap charge, arm-leg synchronization, read block, fight pressure, react when a single defender versus two blockers.

Procedure: (1) For delivering an explosive blow, offensive men line up with their inside knees on the ground or on hands and knees, shoulder-to-shoulder, with the defender in the gap opposite them. Manager is behind offensive blockers in gap facing defensive player, who will then explode into the target with his shoulder on manager's hand signal. As contact is made, he whips his tail down, with his legs extended straight, as blow is completed. After getting the feeling of "popping" or exploding, without first raising up or drawing back, defender repeats drill, then brings his feet up under him, moving them hard and fast and holding in a position ready to react to the offensive linemen's defender, facing blockers, indicating by hand signals their defensive actions and starting count. Drill is then live and defender must learn to read blockers and react to their blocks. Manager (facing defender) signals whether he should try to split the blockers to getting penetration, use goal line- or short-yardage charge, fake penetration, go over the top, play one man, etc.

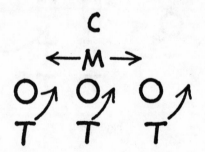

Figure 4-3

Coaching Points: In exploding, stress first move is forward. Do not draw back or raise up. Stress good stance, extending body, vicious flipper, reading block, reacting, speed, quickness, moving feet. Spin-out technique explained previously. On gap technique, defender drives hard and low but at last second turns shoulders and body so that belly is to the ball and then scrambles through the gap. On goal-line and short-yardage technique, defender aims lower, penetrates, grabs ankles, knees, and fights upward. Occasionally permit defender to fake penetration, and/or go over the blockers if he has the ability to do so. Also loop, slant or veer into one blocker (simulated coordinated defense), then react accordingly to the blockers.

8. Defensive Reaction Sled Drill (Figure 4-4)

Purpose: To teach the technique needed to meet offensive charge from lineman, one man to the left or right.

Procedure: Coach fires machine, athlete from 3- or 4-point stance reacts to sled action with cross step and meets attacking pad with shoulder farthest away from attack and then brings front leg around and squares up in gap outside of offensive charge.

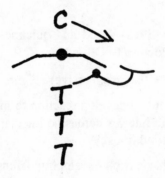

Figure 4-4

Coaching Points: Stress quick reaction. Forearm blow must drive the attacking pad back into lock-set position. Defender must step around to fill gap and square up.

9. Around-the-Circle Hitting Drill (Figure 4-5)

Purpose: To develop arm-leg synchronization from a semiupright position in delivering a blow to warding off a blocker, and destroying the block; and to give the defender a feeling of "hitting."

Procedure: Blockers line up in a semiupright stance in a circle facing clockwise. Defender is inside of the circle in a semiupright stance, working counterclockwise. He synchronizes throwing the forearm with the proper (right) foot forward as he meets limited resistance, pushes off, sprints to the next blocker and repeats procedure around the circle. After each defender has his turn, the drill is repeated, with the defender going around the outside of the circle using the opposite (left) forearm and foot forward.

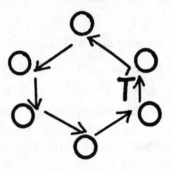

Figure 4-5

Coaching Points: Stress speed and quickness and proper arm-leg synchronization. A follow-up to Drills Nos. 8, 9, 10 and 14, Chapter 2.

10. 1-Versus-3 Drills (progressive) (Figure 4-6)

Purpose: To teach and develop reaction to movements of the three offensive linemen in the interior defensive lineman's area, like those he will face under game conditions.

Procedure: Emphasis is on developing defensive fundamentals and techniques for the interior linemen, especially for the tackles in an even defensive alignment. Coach stands behind the defender, facing the offensive linemen and ball carrier, and indicates with hands, starting count and (a) single cutoff block right or left, (b) leadpost block right or left, (c) wedge block, (d) drop-back pass block, and (e) influence block by offensive player directly across from defender, simulating the trap block from the opposite side and/or (f) the reverse shoulder or straight shoulder block by either offensive lineman to the right and left of the defender. Ball carrier takes path indicated by coach so that defender can locate the ball, pursue and tackle (tag), after having moved on movement and protected his territory first.

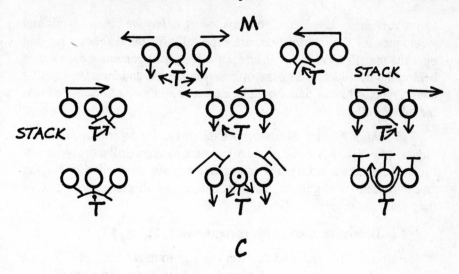

Figure 4-6

Coaching Points: Stress proper defensive fundamentals and techniques. May give down and distance situation to make drill more meaningful. Add fourth blocker as trapper (e).

11. 2-Versus-3 Drills (progressive) (Figure 4-7)

Purpose: To develop reaction to movements of the three offensive linemen in two defenders' areas, like those they will face under game conditions.

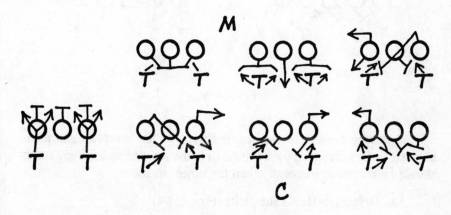

Figure 4-7

Procedure: Emphasis is on developing defensive fundamentals and techniques for the interior linemen, especially for the defenders playing opposite the offensive guards in an even defensive alignment. Coach stands behind the defender, facing the offensive linemen, and indicates starting count, type of blocks that should be executed and path of offensive men, including ball carrier.

Coaching Points: Stress proper defensive fundamentals and techniques. May give down and distance situation to make drill more meaningful, as defenders seldom play head-up in every situation when employing an even defensive alignment. Then defenders may offset to either crack, as they would in a game situation.

12. Defensive Line Drills (progressive) (Figure 4-8)

Purpose: To teach and develop reaction to movements of offensive linemen, like those defensive linemen will face under game conditions.

Procedure: Emphasis is on developing defensive fundamentals and techniques for the interior linemen from tackle to tackle, plus the linebackers in 6-Versus-7 Drills.

Figure 4-8

Coaching Points: Stress proper defensive fundamentals and techniques. The primary purpose of the drill is the reaction to the trap, and it should be run more frequently than the other situations.

13. Defensive Half-Line Drill (Figure 4-4)

Purpose: To recognize, and defend against, the opposition's favorite running and passing plays.

Procedure: The emphasis is on perfecting defensive fundamentals and techniques and recognizing the opposition's favorite plays. Half of the offensive and defensive lines are used. One unit works right, and the other unit left, with the No. 1 and No. 2 defensive units divided up to work half-line at a time. Offense is limited to opposition's favorite play to each side (right or left), and counters and reverses are not run unless they hit inside the off guard on the back side. Use opposition's starting cadence and snap-count.

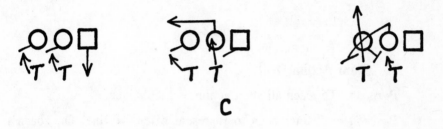

C

Figure 4-9

Coaching Points: Stress good execution by the offense in order to aid recognition and to get good reaction by the defensive units. Change defensive alignments. Rotate off-side guard, middle guard and linebackers so they can practice working both right and left. Drill is live. Use whistle. Give opposition's offensive tendencies, including down, distance and position on the field. Move the ball from the middle of the field to each hash mark.

14. Pursuit Drill (Figure 4-10)

Purpose: To teach and develop the proper angles of pursuit against running plays.

Procedure: Take proper stance, position, alignment, and keys and adhere to the defensive principles of move on movement, etc. The quarterback takes the snap from center and either rolls out right or left, attempts to go up the middle, or drops straight back to pass. He continues to run until every lineman has tagged him or the coach blows the whistle to stop pursuit. The drill is live for the defense, except for tackling. You use a back to each side and pitch to him for sweep effect. Or a wide receiver for sideline pursuit.

Coaching Points: Stress proper angles of pursuit and sprinting to get to the ball carrier to tag him. Change to different defensive alignments.

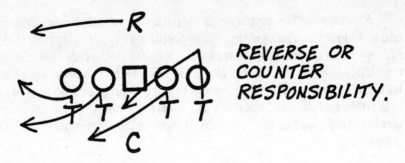

Figure 4-10

15. Stunt Action Drill

Purpose: To teach all stunt action and technique.

Procedure: Set up bags to represent offensive line. On coach's command, defense reacts through or around bags, using proper technique and going for the first 3 to 5 steps of the movement.

Coaching Points: Very important that there is no hesitation in movement or reaction to any stunt called. Correct this immediately. Techniques are worked on in other drills.

16. Pass Rush-and-Peel Drill (Figure 4-11)

Purpose: To teach and develop rushing the passer, and then peeling back in the event of an interception or pass completion.

Procedure: May be used as a pass rush-and-peel drill, in which defenders must rush the passer (coach) when he raises the football signaling, "Pass!" which is recognized and identified immediately. Rushers extend arms upward as they approach the passer, they never jump unless ball is actually thrown, they then attempt to deflect the ball or block the pass if possible. Passer throws the ball, and one of the three stationary receivers downfield catches it. If he sounds off with the interception signal, "Bingo!," the rushers peel back for the return. If he does not sound off after catching the ball, it means the pass has been completed and the rushers must sprint back to catch the receiver as he jogs toward the goal line.

Coaching Points: Stress peeling back to the same side, if ball is thrown to your side. If ball is thrown to opposite side away from where defender rushes, he should continue on through his course of peeling back. If ball is thrown down the middle, indicate whether rusher should turn and peel or continue on through to the opposite side and then peel.

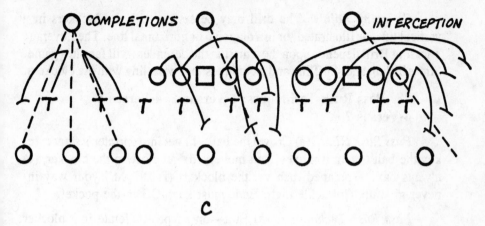

Figure 4-11

17. Leverage Drill (Figure 4-12)

Purpose: To develop warding off and shedding blockers, maintaining leverage and keeping QB in the pocket.

Procedure: Diagram illustrates linebacker or end, but any interior defender may be used in the drill by using a hand shiver (or forearm block by the end) to ward off the first blocker, moving laterally to ward off the second until he tackles or tags the ball carrier. Drill may be half- or full-speed, with the blockers or coach controlling the flow. As soon as the first blocker charges, the second leaves, then the third. The defender must hit, shuffle, hit, shuffle, hit—and maintain leverage on the ball carrier.

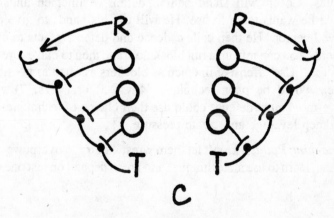

Figure 4-12

Coaching Points: The drill may be set up with the blockers in a vertical line, as illustrated, or in a diagonal or horizontal line. The Leverage Tackling Drill depends upon the situation the defenders will face in a game. Stress hitting and shuffling and techniques, not wrestling with the blockers.

18. Pass Rush Techniques: 1-Versus-1; 4-Versus-5 4-Versus-7

Pass Rush Hints: (a) Crowd the ball; (b) get into sprinter's stance; (c) key the ball (when it moves, you move); (d) get close to the blocker; (e) always have a planned rush vs. the blocker; (f) "Fight" your way in, never give up; (g) tackle high. Ends must keep QB in the pocket.

Pass Rush Techniques: (a) Butt—on snap, accelerate into blocker with forehead (class headgear) and double-hand shiver to drive him backwards; (b) Kung Fu—get close to blocker; grab shoulder pad either side with one hand, pull toward you, turning his shoulders; swing opposite arm across blocker's body (swim), follow with your body to get by blocker; (c) Hook and spin—attack one side of blocker, getting him to turn his shoulders; get close to blocker; as blocker opens to that side, thrust elbow to rear and spin your body to opposite side, using elbow and arm to pull yourself by blocker; push off of blocker's back or side; (d) Race horse—race straight through outside shoulder of blocker after giving inside head fake; if contact is made, slide by his outside by turning your shoulders; don't break stride.

Purpose: To develop good pass rush techniques.

Procedure: Walk through each technique a step at a time with all defensive linemen. Use situation (1 on 1) (4 on 5) (4 on 7) to practice live techniques. Coach will stand behind defensive linemen and call out technique he wants them to use. He will use his hands to give count to offensive linemen. He then calls cadence and defense reacts to offensive movement. You can mix up a run block now and then to make sure defense is on its toes. Use offensive linemen as blockers as often as possible. The next step would be open technique (4 vs. 5) or (4 vs. 7) when an offensive-movement defense could use their choice of techniques as long as they keep leverage and create pressure.

Coaching Points: Don't let them wrestle or try to overpower people. Make them learn to use all techniques and not to depend on just one or two.

Chapter 5

LINEBACKING FUNDAMENTALS AND TECHNIQUES

THE REAL SOUL OF ANY DEFENSE IS GOOD LINEBACK-ING. There never has been a strong defensive team with incapable linebackers. A team must have good linebacking in order to have a strong defense. You should expect your linebackers to lead the team in tackles every year. In building a defensive unit, consideration must be given to the selection of your best athletes for the linebacking positions. They must be your most aggressive players. They need to have a feel for the game: you can't teach this, you have to find the athletes who possess it and make them linebackers.

NECESSARY INHERENT QUALITIES AND SKILLS

Consideration should be given to the following physical qualifications, technical skills and inherent qualities in selecting linebacking personnel.

Middle Linebacker

1. *Good size and aggressiveness.*

Size is essential, since the linebacker will not only move up into the line on occasion, but must meet the play in the hole at the line of scrimmage. A small- or medium-sized linebacker, although an excellent tackler, does not have the physical toughness and durability to meet the interference and ball carrier consistently when filling the holes opened in the defensive line. He simply cannot stand up under the physical pounding and strain, and is likely to be injured frequently.

The small-sized linebacker is also handicapped by the fact that on such plays he will seldom stop the ball carrier without at least a couple of yards gained, even when he meets the play at the line of scrimmage. A good point-of-attack back generally gains some yardage hitting the line, and it takes a linebacker with good size and concentrated "hitting power" to minimize the gain.

Ability comes in any size and, contrary to the previous statements, an individual should not be excluded merely because of lack of size *if* he is hard-nosed, likes to tackle, and has the other qualities and skills the position demands. This is especially true if employing stunting defenses and the linebacker is quick.

Outside Linebackers

Size is not a factor here to the extent it is on the inside. These players must be able to cover fast backs one-on-one in passing situations. They must also be able to pursue effectively from one side of the field to the other. Quickness and speed are strong qualities here that can offset size to some extent.

2. *Competitiveness.*

Great football players are usually strong competitors, have confidence in themselves and their ability, and generally possess qualities of leadership. If consideration is given initially to selecting several of the best defensive players as linebackers, it is likely they will possess these inherent qualities to some extent.

Since linebackers are usually the leaders of the defensive team, the position demands players who must be tough mentally as well as physically. They must be willing to assume the responsibilities of leadership.

3. *Good football sense.*

Through repetitious drill, most players can be taught play recognition and offensive tendencies. Comprehension of this information is important in order to attain maximum results in defensing the opposition's running and passing offense. Linebackers should be able to diagnose the opposition's plays quickly and surely, and then react immediately to the play. They must also read changes in the offensive sets and be able to adjust the defensive call from the sideline.

Since the signal caller (linebacker) controls the defensive strategy, he should know the defensive alignment and assignment of every teammate. The linebacker is in position to see the offensive alignment and deployment of personnel, he must be taught to recognize the variations and, if necessary, to check out of one defense and into another one adjusting to the offense. If the defensive linemen have trouble adjusting to unusual splits and surprise formations, it is the linebacker's responsibility to help his teammates in their alignment, and to compensate for improper adjustments. In making a quick adjustment, the linebackers must clearly indicate their exact responsibilities to the other people involved.

4. *Reaction skills.*

The typical linebacker should be a combination of a defensive back and lineman. Since under normal conditions he is part of the forcing defense, he must be able to handle the running play to his area. If the play does not hit in his area, then he must keep himself free and maintain proper leverage on the ball carrier.

A linebacker does not have to possess great speed, but he should have first-step quickness. Assuming he is reading and not stunting, he must react and move quickly after reading his key, without first false-stepping. On almost every offensive play, someone will try to block the linebacker. He must be able to shed or ward off blockers quickly and react to the ball.

Pass defenders must react quickly and have good mobility. With more emphasis on the passing game in present-day football, additional attention must be given to the linebacker's ability to defend against the forward pass. The linebacker is an integral part of pass defense whether dropping back to cover a zone or man-for-man, holding up an intended receiver, or putting pressure on the QB.

5. *Taking correct angles of pursuit and good tackling.*

Linebackers must be masters of proper pursuit angles. The good linebackers know the correct angles of pursuit versus every running and pass play. This is another facet of football sense. By studying the opponents on film and knowing their personnel, the linebacker can judge his speed in relation to the ball carrier's. After the front line of defense makes its attack, the linebacker is usually in the best position to make the tackle, which should be near the line of scrimmage. If the ball carrier should get by the linebacker, the latter must change his course and attempt to intercept the runner by using the proper angle of pursuit in a second effort to tackle him.

FUNDAMENTALS AND TECHNIQUES OF
LINEBACKER'S STANCE

It is important for the linebacker to take the proper stance and the correct alignment so that he can come into an effective "hitting position" and react properly when the play begins. While his stance and individual alignment will depend upon such factors as the defensive alignment, tactical situation, and reads, etc., fundamentally, a good football stance for the linebacker is as follows:

1. Semiupright two-point stance with the weight equally distributed on the balls of the feet, approximately shoulder-width, toes pointed straight ahead, feet parallel, and either even or slightly staggered. If in the latter position, the inside foot should be in advance of the outside foot in a toe-to-instep or heel relationship, depending upon which feels the most comfortable to the linebacker.

The positioning of the feet depends on the individual coach, and what he wants the linebacker to accomplish. Regardless of the foot position, it is imperative for the linebacker to meet the blocker firing out at him with the inside foot forward.

2. The knees are flexed slightly, and point straight ahead.

3. The hips are flexed, body crouched slightly, in a comfortable position.

4. The shoulders should be parallel with the line of scrimmage, and the arms should hang straight down with a slight bend at the elbows. The hands are generally clenched, but relaxed. The hands or elbows should not be placed on the knees or thighs.

5. The head and eyes should be in a position for the linebacker to see his key. His stance should be such that his line of vision will be nearly parallel to the ground as he reads his key, reacting immediately to it.

LINEBACKER'S POSITION AND
ALIGNMENT TECHNIQUES

It is imperative for the linebacker to take his correct lateral and vertical alignment in order to operate with maximum efficiency. In a normal situation with the offensive line taking regular splits, the linebacker's lateral position in the normal alignment will be shading the outside ear, head-up of the center and in the Wide Tackle 6 alignment, on the outside ear of the offensive tackle. By taking a nose-ear alignment, the linebacker's inside foot will approximately split the crotch of the offensive man opposite whom he is playing. Fundamentally this is his alignment, which may change before the ball is put into play depending on the tactical situation, the offensive set, tendencies, how extended motion is covered, pass coverage called, defensive stunt on. Linebackers should always shade to the strength of the offensive formation.

Fundamentally the linebacker's vertical position will be approximately 3 to 5 yards off the line of scrimmage, although his depth depends on such personnel factors as how deep he can play and still hold his ground, and how tight he can play and still support at the corner, and get back on passes. The tactical situation is always a determining factor and can never be discounted. In a short-yardage situation, excluding the other tactical factors, the linebacker normally will move closer to the line of scrimmage. Conversely on long yardage, the linebacker normally will loosen so interior linemen cannot legally fire out and block him on a pass play. He is also closer to covering his pass responsibility. A general rule in a long-yardage situation, without considering the entire tactical situation, is for the linebacker to play off the line of scrimmage approximately half as far as the distance to be gained by the offensive team. Loosening to a depth of 4 to 5 yards would probably be sufficient, depending upon the tactical situation and the linebacker's assignment.

As part of the forcing unit of the defense, the linebacker must be able to handle the running play to his area first. If the run does not hit in his area, then he must free himself and move to the ball. He should stop inside plays, and pursue the wide plays from inside-out. He must move at an angle which will put him in front of the ball carrier.

In the even defense, unless stunting, most coaches have the linebackers key and react to the movements of the offensive guards, and the football; and in the Wide Tackle 6, to the offensive tackles opposite the linebackers.

In practice drills versus a skeleton offense, most linebackers will watch their keys and react favorably. When working against a full offensive unit, however, the linebackers will often forget their keys and watch the action of the offensive backs. They must be drilled to watch their keys, and read them properly in order to operate with maximum efficiency. By watching the backfield action, the linebacker can be pulled out of position by the back movement of the offensive play. This neutralizes and destroys the linebacker's aggressiveness and effectiveness.

There are different points of view as to whether an offensive lineman or back offers the best key for the linebacker. Many coaches believe the offensive guard or tackle furnishes the best key for the linebacker when the defense is played straight, and is not stunting, since the guard or tackle will indicate the play quicker than any other key. Other coaches want the linebacker to look into the offensive backfield for his key, generally keying the nearest back, regardless of whether he is playing the defense straight or stunting. Many offenses force you to cross-key on the backs.

COACHING POINTS FOR LINEBACKERS

Additional coaching points and defensive principles for linebackers are as follows:

1. In a definite passing situation, loosen up, unless assigned to hold up an offensive end. In an obvious passing situation, look for a screen pass or the draw play. Some teams like to run a trap play up the middle in this situation.

2. When playing over an end, never allow him to release and run out unmolested for a pass. Throw off the timing of the pass by striking and shoving the receiver, forcing him to alter his pass route or direction. The linebacker must be careful not to grab the receiver's face mask. He may harass the receiver until the ball leaves the passer's hand, as long as the receiver is in front of him.

3. Offensive linemen generally tip a drop-back pass by showing passive blocking or a retreating type of block protection immediately. The linebacker should yell "Pass!" when he is convinced it is a pass, and assume pass responsibility. If the passer drops back, slows up, then fades again, the linebacker should yell "Pass!" then "Screen!" and assume screen pass responsibility. While the linebacker generally is not responsible for the draw play, if the quarterback goes back as if to pass but hands off to another back, the linebacker should yell "Draw!" and move in to tackle the ball carrier. Communication is very important.

4. When a pass is thrown, break for and play the football. Be aggressive on pass defense, as the football belongs to whoever wants it. The linebacker should attempt to get in front of the ball before it is released from the passer's hand. This forces the passer either to throw over the linebacker, attempt to drill the ball by him, or to alter his throw.

5. On an interception yell "Bingo!," pass it down the line. If the linebacker is nearest the man for whom the pass was intended, he should block back on him. Otherwise, he hustles to get in front of the teammate who has caught the pass, throwing a block at the first opponent who threatens the runback of the interception.

6. After penetrating across the line of scrimmage against a well-executed action pass fake, which then develops into a pass, continue to rush

the passer and force the play. It is almost impossible to recover quickly enough to be effective downfield as a pass defender, under such circumstances.

7. When firing or "stunting" do so on the snap of the ball. Then play as a lineman after penetrating the line of scrimmage, sliding with the running play and accelerating your rush if a pass develops.

8. When the territory between the tackle and end is the linebacker's responsibility and the block of the offensive end indicates an off-tackle play, the linebacker should guard against penetrating too deeply into the hole and getting trapped by the interference thus widening the hole. Assuming he is not stunting or firing, if the linebacker meets the play in the hole and makes the tackle he will have done his job effectively.

9. On running plays to the opposite side or when the flow is away, the off-side linebacker should look for the ball carrier cutting back inside of the on-side linebacker, or for the delayed receiver cutting across for the pass. In the latter case, the linebacker should attempt to knock off the intended receiver, not permitting the latter to get behind him.

DRILLS FOR THE LINEBACKER

Since good linebacking demands players with agility, reaction, mobility, etc., as was discussed previously, drills for the linebackers should incorporate the teaching of these qualities, fundamentals and skills. The following agility and/or reaction drills are excellent for the linebacker: Carioca, Follow-the-Leader, High Stepper, Running-the-Line, Wave, Crab, and Quarter-Eagle.

Since the linebacker will be knocked off his feet at times, he should be drilled in getting up off the ground for a second effort and reaction. Such drills as Forward Rolls, Somersaults, Shoulder Rolls, Log Rolls, and others of a similar nature are excellent, especially if a second reaction is incorporated in the drill. After executing a roll, the linebacker should regain his feet and then ward off or shed a blocker, react, pursue and tackle so that a single drill may be employed to teach several reactions and techniques. Since many of these drills have been explained and illustrated already in other chapters, they will not be repeated here.

It is not unusual, when training the linebacker, that he will be able to tell you whom he keys and how he should react to his key, but he will be unable to react properly. The complete coordination of eye, mind and body can be accomplished only through repetitive drill.

Tackling drills should always be completed first. They are discussed and diagrammed in the tackling chapter (Chapter 3).

1. Key-Reaction Drills—Shoulder in Front (Figure 5-1)

Purpose: To teach proper alignment, keys and reaction to (A) key firing out straight; (B) key blocking to his right; (C) key blocking to his left; (D) key pulling to his right; (E) key pulling to his left; and (F) key setting up for dropback pass block.

Procedure: Each section of the drill is done separately and until the linebacker becomes proficient; then all of the reactions are combined into one drill so that the linebacker does not know in advance the movement his key is going to make. When the drill is run as a combined drill, the coach stands behind the linebacker facing the offensive linemen and flashes his movement to him, along with the starting count. Coach calls snap number, and as key moves linebacker reacts as has been described in detail in this chapter.

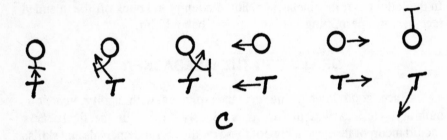

Figure 5-1

Coaching Points: Stress proper alignment, and maintaining proper alignment. Do not permit false-stepping, and check proper angle of pursuit. In (D) and (E) indicate to linebacker whether he is an on-side or off-side linebacker, and practice both. Coach each phase thoroughly progressing to the combined drill.

2. Defensive Reaction Drill

Purpose: To teach reaction to cutoff or angle block.

Procedure: Put linebacker in proper stance 1 yard in front of D.R. sled. Coach will fire machine off and linebacker must react with opposite shoulder and foot. Cross-step in front of pad, forearm blast to pad and step around and square up to hole.

Coaching Points: Stress good stance and fast reaction time. Make him force the pad back into locked position. The step around and squaring up is the most important. Striking a good blow is of no use unless he follows up and fills the hole.

3. Hit-Hit-Hit Drill (Figure 5-2)

Purpose: To teach and develop delivering a blow in order to destroy the offensive man's block.

Procedure: Linebacker takes his proper alignment laterally, with both players in the "ready" position. Blocker steps toward linebacker, who jab-steps and throws forearm, simulating the aggressive technique described previously in delivering a blow to destroy the block. Blocker steps back and comes again, and linebacker recoils and uncoils again three times. Both men "bounce" up and back, with the linebacker practicing delivering a controlled blow to the chest of the blocker. The linebacker moves to the other shoulder and repeats the drill three times, simulating that the block is coming from outside-in, whereas the other block was from inside-out. He should not reverse the position of his feet if using a staggered stance, but must deliver the blow with same shoulder and foot forward, especially when the blocker is coming from outside-in.

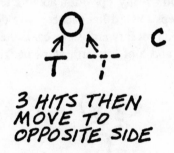

3 HITS THEN
MOVE TO
OPPOSITE SIDE

Figure 5-2

Coaching Points: Stress proper fundamentals and techniques of delivering a blow to destroy the block. Control drill so that emphasis is on quickness and arm-leg synchronization.

4. Hit-Shuffle-Hit Drill (Figure 5-3)

Purpose: To teach and develop delivering a blow to destroy the offensive man's block.

Procedure: Linebacker in "ready" position, "hits" with right shoulder, shuffles laterally to his right, and hits with left shoulder, shuffles laterally to his left, hits with right shoulder, three times with each shoulder for six reactions. Players bounce in, out, shuffle, etc.

Figure 5-3

Coaching Points: Stress proper fundamentals of delivering a blow, and proper arm-leg synchronization. No false-stepping.

5. Bounce Drill (Figure 5-4)

Purpose: To teach and develop delivering a blow, and arm-leg synchronization.

Procedure: Offensive men in semiupright position 12 to 18 inches apart, and linebacker in "ready" position about 2 feet from blockers. The one blocker (right) steps toward linebacker, who delivers a blow to him with same shoulder and foot forward, steps back, steps toward left blocker with proper shoulder and foot forward, steps back. Repeat six times.

Figure 5-4

Coaching Points: Stress proper arm-leg synchronization, and have players bounce up and back. Linebacker must step back after delivering a blow each time.

6. Pyramid Drill (Figure 5-5)

Purpose: To teach and develop delivering a blow and arm-leg synchronization.

Procedure: Same as Bounce Drill, only coach stands behind linebackers and indicates which blocker is to attack him. Linebacker starts from "ready" position, jab-steps to meet blocker with proper shoulder and foot, returns to original position ready to meet either blocker again. Repeat six times.

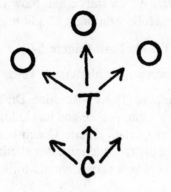

Figure 5-5

Coaching Points: Stress proper arm-leg synchronization. Linebacker must recoil each time after delivering a blow.

7. Sled Drills (2 & 7 man) (Figure 5-6)

Purpose: To develop good forearm and hand shiver techniques.

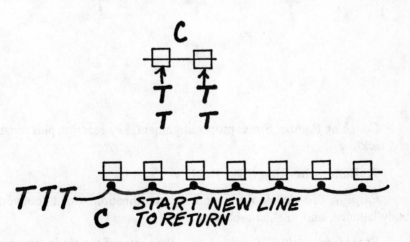

Figure 5-6

Procedure: (2-man sled) 2 linebackers at a time; on coach's command athletes will take proper step from good stance and deliver a strong blow (forearm or hand) to raise the pads and sled. (7-man sled) on coach's command athlete slides down the sled striking a good blow (forearm or hand) to teach pad from a good stance.

Coaching Points: Watch stance and blow techniques. Make them use maximum force and follow through. Conditioning can occur here, also.

8. Key-React-Tackle Drill (Figure 5-7)

Purpose: To teach proper alignment, keys, reaction.

Procedure: Same as (1) Key-Reaction Drill, only a ball carrier is added so that linebacker can pursue and tackle him. Linebacker assumes "ready" position in proper alignment. Coach is facing blocker and ball carrier, but behind linebacker, and indicates starting count, movement of lineman, and hole where ball carrier should hit.

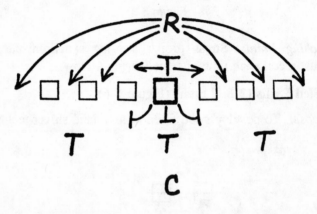

Figure 5-7

Coaching Points: Stress proper alignment, key-reaction plus pursuit and tackling.

9. Bull-in-the-Ring Shed Drill

Purpose: To develop arm and leg coordination, rapid footwork, body balance, and to shed a blocker.

Procedure: "Bull" (linebacker) in the center of the circle, pumping arms and legs, and moving in a counterclockwise direction slowly. (1) Bull can point at the blocker who he wants to attack him. (2) Coach can indicate the blocker. (3) Blocker can come on own from the rim and try to drive the linebacker out of the circle with a running shoulder block. Bull meets blockers, one at a time, synchronizing proper arm-leg and delivering a blow to the blocker with force. He should shed the blocker, using the techniques explained previously, and continue to turn to meet another blocker. Four or five repetitions will be sufficient before replacing linebacker in the middle.

Coaching Points: If either of first two methods is used, the blocker to either side of the one indicated may come in order to get a better reaction. (Explain method before drill starts.) If blockers come on own, man who is coming should yell "Here!" before charging "Bull." Stress quickness, proper arm-leg action, and shedding blocker immediately. Do not wrestle with blocker. Alternate forearm-shoulder lifts so linebacker cannot favor strength and protect weakness. No clipping from behind.

10. Machine Gun Drill (Figure 5-8)

Purpose: To develop arm and leg coordination, and to shed blockers.

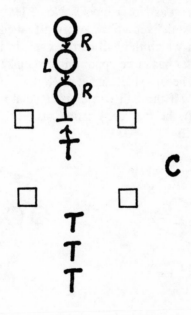

Figure 5-8

Procedure: Upright dummies are set up inside a 5-yard square forming an approximately-3-yard box. The linebacker assumes a "ready" position a foot inside of the front line of his box. The blockers line up in a column a yard off the line outside the box. The coach regulates the flow of blockers so that the linebacker must ward off and shed the blockers just as fast as the coach sends them. The linebacker tries to keep from being driven out of the box, and must ward off men with his hands, knees, elbows, forearms, depending on how quickly the blockers come at him. If knocked down, the linebacker must get up immediately and keep fighting to shed men as the coach continues to send blockers at him.

Coaching Points: Stress quickness and meeting blockers from the front. Do not get spun around and turn back on flow or direction of blockers coming in the front of the box. Blockers should not clip from behind if linebacker gets turned around. When blocker gets even or beyond linebacker, he should go out the rear of the box. Control piling on by regulating flow of blockers if linebacker is knocked off his feet.

11. Leverage or Outside Shed Drill (Figure 5-9)

Purpose: To develop shedding the blockers, pursuit and tackling.

Procedure: Drill is either one-half or full-speed, with blockers regulating flow. As soon as No. 1 blocks, No. 2 leaves, then No. 3. Linebacker (or end) must deliver a blow, ward off, shed and make the tackle. Restrict the area in which the ball carrier can run laterally, favoring the linebacker. The latter has more opportunity to make the tackle if blockers must pull and block because ball carrier has further to run to evade him, and drill is not as fast. If the ball carrier is lined up 4 yards opposite the linebacker (or end), he can get outside faster. Linebacker must react quicker in latter drill.

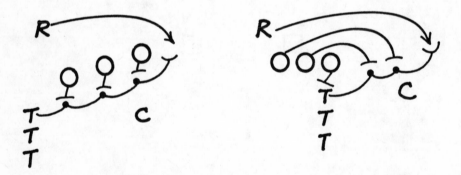

Figure 5-9

Coaching Points: Stress taking inside-out pursuit, maintaining proper leverage. Drill may be set up with blockers in a vertical, horizontal or diagonal line.

12. Inside Shed Drill (Figure 5-10)

Purpose: To develop reaction to key firing out straight, delivering a blow, shedding the blocker, and tackling.

Procedure: On starting count blocker fires out at linebacker. Ball carrier is at a depth of 4 yards, and approaches rear of blocker slowly, then breaks. Linebacker must deliver a blow to the blocker, destroying his block, shed him, and make the tackle. Second linebacker may be added to polish off the ball carrier, if used as a tackling drill. (Or this may be used as a tackling drill by having a defensive lineman nose-on the blocker on the line, with or without the linebacker stacked behind him.)

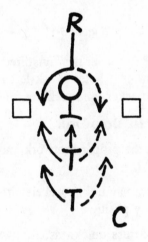

Figure 5-10

Coaching Points: If 1-on-1, have the linebacker in proper alignment (nose-on-ear) and not nose-on-nose (as illustrated). Stress proper fundamentals of maintaining position, jab-step and forearm lift, shed, tackling.

13. Eye-Opener Drill (Figure 5-11)

Purpose: To teach maintaining proper leverage on the ball carrier, shedding the blocker, and tackling.

Procedure: Upright dummies are placed on a straight line, allowing 5 feet between each dummy. Linebacker is in a "ready" position at one of the dummies, across from a blocker and a ball carrier who is 3 yards behind him. Blocker tells ball carrier which hole he is going to lead him through, and the ball carrier must go into that hole. Coach flips the football to the ball carrier, who follows his blocker. The linebacker meets the blocker in the hole, sheds him, and makes the tackle from an inside-out position, driving his head across and in front of the ball carrier.

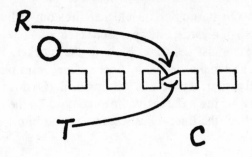

Figure 5-11

Coaching Points: Ball carrier may run directly into the hole, or fake once and go through the next hole. Work left and right. Stress proper leverage, shedding the blocker, and tackling fundamentals.

14. Linebacker Pass Drop Drill

Purpose: To teach the proper footwork and angles of drop for the linebackers.

Procedure: On command, linebackers drop to pass zones using proper footwork and body position.

Coaching Points: Stress quickness, footwork (don't cross legs or turn back to ball) and good drop angles.

15. Ball Drill

Purpose: To teach and develop breaking at the proper angle (90°) on a straight line to intercept the ball thrown to either side of the defender.

Procedure: Using a marked-off area, the linebacker sets up at 10 yards, and the passer 5 to 6 yards, from the line of scrimmage so there is a distance of 15 to 16 yards between the two players. The passer raises the ball, indicating pass, and linebacker yells "Pass!" Passer throws the ball to the right or left of the linebacker, who must break at a 90° angle for the ball in order to reach the interception point. On catching the ball, linebacker sounds off with interception signal, "Bingo!" or some other designated word.

Coaching Points: In *all* drills, defender yells "Pass!" as soon as pass is indicated, and the appropriate interception signal when he or a teammate catches the ball. Build confidence of the linebacker by first throwing the ball directly to his right or left, and work outward until linebacker can react quickly, go on a straight line, and intercept the pass thrown approximately 8 yards plus on either side of his position. Check his feet so he does not run in an arc for the interception. Catch football at its height, not when it is descending, and with the fingertips.

16. Pass Drop and Ball Drill (Figure 5-12)

Purpose: To teach and develop breaking at the proper angle on a straight line in order to intercept the ball thrown to either side of the defender.

Procedure: Same setup as Going-for-the-Ball Drill, only passer and linebacker are approximately 10 yards apart, and two receivers are added, who are 5 yards apart (working outward until they are 15 yards apart). Passer takes two short steps backward and raises the football. Linebacker drop-steps with outside foot first, and then crosses over with inside foot and squares off so he is facing the passer when the latter raises the ball. He is in a "ready" position and breaks to intercept the pass when it is thrown. Linebacker must sound off when ball is raised.

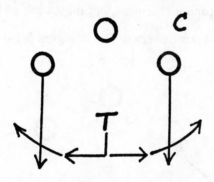

Figure 5-12

Coaching Points: Stress immediate rotation of hips and reaction to the ball.

17. Chugging Receivers Drill (Figure 5-13)

Purpose: To "chug" receiver, holding him up, and still cover area of responsibility on pass defense.

Procedure: Linebackers take Eagle alignment on inside shoulder of ends, as illustrated, or head-up over the ends on the 5-3, 4-3 alignments.

Do not permit receivers to release inside, but attempt to hold them up at the line of scrimmage. If ends are forced to release outside, they should still run a hook at 12 yards. Linebackers must cover their hook zones at 10 yards, and passer must throw the football before receivers get a depth of 15 yards.

Figure 5-13

Coaching Points: Defenders must use legal tactics to chug receivers and hold them up. Force ends outside, with defenders turning to the outside facing the ends when going back to their hook zones. Slide after getting to hook zone. Passer cannot fake pass, but must cock and throw.

18. Man-for-Man Coverage Drill (Figure 5-14)

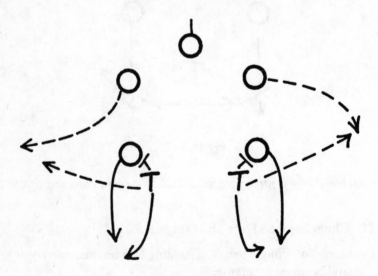

Figure 5-14

Purpose: To teach man-for-man pass coverage.

Procedure: Linebackers are assigned man-for-man coverage on the remaining backs. Passer sets up to pass. If key (back) sets up to block, linebacker covers hook zone on his side and is "free." If key releases and goes out for a pass, or sets up and then releases, linebacker has him man-for-man. Passer should throw quickly and not try to beat linebacker deep with halfback down the middle, although linebacker must attempt to cover receiver deep. If key (back) comes to the inside through the line, linebacker "chugs" him and stays with his man.

Coaching Points: Stress watching key and taking off quickly with him. Throw flares, swings, and cover motion man-for-man.

19. Defender's Net Drill (Figure 5-15)

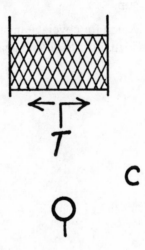

Figure 5-15

Purpose: To teach and develop breaking on a straight line to intercept the pass thrown to either side.

Procedure: Net covering the goal posts is used, only linebacker is head-on the center, keying the quarterback, and the line of scrimmage is the 5 yard line. Quarterback takes snap-back and goes to the pocket to set up for a drop-back pass. Linebacker uses drop-step, crossover sprint back technique to set up in a good defensive football position in the middle of the net approximately 15 yards from the passer. Passer can throw the ball anywhere inside the posts and under the crossbar, and the linebacker must break at a 90° angle on a straight line to intercept the pass.

Coaching Points: Linebacker must stop and set up when passer stops. Check false-stepping, and running in an arc. Passer cannot fake as linebacker is playing the first throwing motion.

20. 7-on-7 Drill

Purpose: To teach proper coverage techniques against offense to be faced that week.

Procedure: Set up a scout offensive team that will run the pass offense of your next opponent from their sets. Use the coverages your scouting reports have indicated will be most effective against this opponent. Have them run each pass pattern 2 to 3 times from each set against your first and second group.

Coaching Points: Watch for coverage mistakes or defensive adjustments that need to be made in order to defend against your next opponent.

Chapter 6

DEFENSIVE SECONDARY
FUNDAMENTALS
AND TECHNIQUES

Secondary defenders must be able to move and react, fight a receiver for the football, and make the tackle in the open field. These skills may be taught through repetitive drills. However, such drills are of little value if the defender lacks a burning desire to play pass defense. A good defensive back not only wants to intercept every pass that is thrown in his area, but he wants to make the tackle as close as possible to the line of scrimmage on running plays. Therefore, he must know well the responsibilities and duties of his position, and react properly with quickness and speed.

DEFENSIVE SECONDARY FUNDAMENTALS

The basic fundamentals for defensive secondary play include the following:

1. Stance.
2. Alignments: position on the field, depth and defense.
3. Responsibilities and coverage: on passes, on running plays, angle of pursuit, rotation, and reaction to keys.
3. Tackling: coming up on sweeps, open-field, head-on, angle, and gang.

CONCEPTS OF PASS DEFENSE

Reiterating the widely recognized and accepted fact that the one play in football which will defeat a team the quickest is the long pass for the easy touchdown; defensively the objective, then, is to eliminate this play first. The second objective of pass defense is to intercept the pass. A team cannot win without a sound pass defense.

In order to have a good pass defense a coach must sell his players on the type he believes to be the best, whether it is zone, man-for-man, or combination coverage. He must also sell the athletes on themselves. Defensive people must have total confidence in themselves. No matter where their opponents get the ball, they can stop them dead! In addition, a coach must decide whether he is going to rush aggressively, hold up eligible receivers or cover zones (or eligible receivers).

Probably the best pass defense is to rush the passer aggressively, although the defensive signal caller must mix his defenses. He cannot continually give the passer a strong rush, especially "stunting" the linebackers. At least one rusher must get to the passer quickly, with other defenders having definite responsibilities for the screen and draw, and outside containment. It is very important to maintain an outside leverage on the passer.

Secondary Pass Coverage

The defensive secondary must play keys and recognize the opposition's favorite pass cuts and patterns. Generally, the keys are the offensive end and near back to the defender's side of the field, and the football. Any interior lineman releasing downfield indicates a running play, and if they drop back, the secondary defenders should look for a pass. In man-for-man coverage, a secondary defender (including linebackers), has his man all the way if he releases downfield. If his key sets up in a pass block, generally the defender is free to help out in his area, although he is still responsible if a screen pass is thrown to the man he is keying.

There is no defense against the perfectly thrown pass, although its completion is discouraging. Then the opposition must locate the weakness of the defensive alignment and coverage, and attempt to guess correctly in order to exploit your weakness. But by your rushing the passer aggressively, he will be forced to throw the ball quickly and possibly off balance. Both of these factors lead to interceptions. By your delaying or holding up receivers at or near the line of scrimmage, they cannot get into the secondary quickly and they must deviate from their set course or pattern.

Both factors throw off the timing of the pass. The defenders must be in the proper position when covering receivers or zones to intercept the poorly thrown pass.

A secondary defender should have some idea of what the other secondary defenders are doing in order to understand his individual pass-run responsibilities in an alignment. It is likely the defenders will grasp their assignments and understand their responsibilities better if they visualize the whole defense first. This is especially true when various types of coverage are employed by a team against numerous offensive sets.

Position on the Receiver Techniques

If the defender's key releases downfield, the defender should shuffle back in the direction of his area of responsibility (zone) watching the receiver and the passer. He should shuffle back, not sprinting until the receiver gets to approximately 3 yards away from the defender as the latter stays between him and the goal line in his defensive zone. He maintains an outside lateral position of approximately 2 yards on the receiver so that he can look at the passer and see the receiver with peripheral vision. The defender should face outward as long as possible, and not change from side to side in his coverage. When the receiver starts to sprint, the defender should stay with him, running under control, but continuing to face in the same direction as he looks through the receiver to the passer.

Man-for-man coverage. If it is man-for-man coverage, the defender has him all the way and does not release from him until the ball is thrown. He should not expect help in covering his man, although he may receive it if another secondary defender is "free" and does not have a receiver to cover man-for-man.

Zone coverage. If it is zone coverage, the defender will play the deepest receiver in his zone man-for-man, and will not release from him until the opponent goes into another defender's zone or the ball is thrown. If it is the former, the defender notifies his teammate that a receiver is leaving his zone and is going into the teammate's zone. He immediately looks for another opponent coming into his vacated zone as he maintains proper field balance.

As was pointed out previously, in order to have good pass defense defenders must always communicate with each other. They should call out what they see, and keep each other alert, such as, "Pass!" "I've got it!" "Your man!" "My man!" "I've got him!" "You take him!" "Ends crossing!" "Down the middle!" or "Bingo!," *et al.* Communication is as important as any other aspect of the coverage.

Pass Interception Techniques

Pass defense is pride and desire. The defender should try to elim-inate false-stepping when the ball is thrown, so he can release immediately from the would-be receiver or the zone and sprint to the interception point. The defender must be aggressive and go for the football with both hands, playing it through a receiver if necessary in order to get to the ball. He should look the football into his hands, especially on the long pass. He should attempt to catch the football at the highest point he can reach, instead of waiting to catch it on its downward descent. On an interception he should sound off with the interception signal, go to the nearest sideline, and score.

If the ball is thrown into another zone, the defender must converge on the receiver and be in a position to intercept the ball, catch the deflected ball, block for a teammate who intercepts, or tackle the receiver.

All defenders should know the tactical situation, and whether or not it is good strategy to intercept or ground the ball. The technique of grounding a pass that otherwise might be intercepted is to slam the ball to the ground with both hands.

As the ball leaves the passer's hand, all secondary defenders go for the ball regardless of where they are. A defender must react to the ball while it is in the air.

Pass defenders should not follow head, arm or leg fakes, and should not turn their backs on the ball except when they roll back to get depth to sprint to the interception point for the pass thrown behind and beyond them.

The deep backs should always be as deep as the deepest, and as wide as the widest receiver in their zones, and always play the sidelines. A deep defender should never permit a receiver to get behind him. The closer the opposition gets to your goal line, the closer the pass defenders play the intended receivers.

SECONDARY TECHNIQUES VERSUS RUNNING GAME

The proper angle of pursuit is very important, as has been cited previously. Secondary defenders must know the proper angles of pursuit and the fill patterns versus the opposition's running attack.

Depending upon the tactical situation, and assuming there is not a stunt "on" in the defensive secondary, generally a secondary defender will play for a pass first and then react to a running play. Some teams key interior linemen first, such as the center on an even alignment and the offensive guards on an odd alignment, and then shift their attention to the ends and flankers. If the interior linemen do not release downfield, the secondary defenders look for eligible receivers, and react depending upon the type of pass coverage they are employing.

Assuming a team is employing a two-deep (four-deep) secondary and the keys indicate a wide running play, normally with no stunt on the weak corner man away from the flow will rotate back and the strong corner man will rotate up. Since the latter is charged with containment as no stunt is on, the strong corner man must turn the play back to the inside. His play must be aggressive and not be ''soft'' as he cannot permit a running lane to be opened between his outside position and the position of his end teammate on the inside.

The strong safety has an inside fill between his corner man and defensive end. He should make the tackle as near as possible to the line of scrimmage. On an option play he will tackle either the fullback or the quarterback, depending on which one has the ball. He is supported on the inside by his linebackers.

The free safety will rotate over on the flow away from his position and fill from the inside, as will be the case with the weak corner man should the ball carrier get beyond the line of scrimmage. The strong corner man cannot be taken in and must force the play back to the inside in order to set up the proper angles of pursuit and gang tackling for his teammates.

Assuming a team is employing a three-step secondary and the keys indicate a wide running play, the defensive end will try to force the play deep with the strong corner containing it from the outside. The safety fills inside between the strong corner and his end. The principles of proper pursuit are the same as explained previously. The secondary defenders must be sure to take the proper angle of pursuit which will put them in position to tackle the ball carrier.

PASS DEFENSE DRILLS

It is an acknowledged fact that only through drills can a team's pass defense be improved. Through drills, the following basic fundamentals of pass defenses can be taught:

1. Be in the proper position at all times.
2. Increase the interception distance in getting to the ball.
3. Play the football after it is thrown.

Proper position means both positioning the receiver and being in the proper field position when the ball is on either hash mark or in the middle of the field, versus both the flow pass (toward and away) and the drop-back pass. It also includes learning how to sprint going away from the passer, yet keeping head turned and eyes on the passer.

Lengthening the interception distance means changing direction once the ball is thrown, eliminating false-stepping, in order to intercept or get to the ball. The strength of any pass defense will depend on the distance the defenders can move after the ball is thrown.

Playing the football after it is thrown means learning to go after it aggressively, playing it at its height, and through a possible receiver if necessary. The defender should not wait until the football is on its downward course before intercepting it. He should attempt to catch it at the highest point he can reach with arms, hands and fingers extended.

Drills for teaching secondary pass defense fundamentals and techniques are as follows: Each day should start with a series of at least three tackling drills taken from the tackling chapter (Chapter 3).

1. Defensive Wave Drill

Purpose: To improve the individual defender's fundamentals to be in the proper position at all times, increase the interception distance, and to play the football after it is thrown; to improve team pass defense.

Procedure: From a good defensive football position, the three defenders react to the arm motion of the coach, using a crossover step with hip rotation and moving at a diagonal angle backward. When the coach (passer) indicates a change of direction, the defender plants his away (far) foot, pushes off turning to the inside, and uses a crossover step going in the direction indicated. After 4 to 5 reactions, the ball is thrown and the defenders sprint to the interception point, with one man catching the ball and the other two leading interference back to the line of scrimmage.

Coaching Points (for all pass defense drills): Recognize and identify, "Pass!" Sound off with the interception signal, "Block!" ("Bingo!"), and pass it down the line. Sprint to the interception point. Peel back on the intended receiver or lead interference quickly downfield. Stress proper planting procedure. No false-stepping. Catch the football at highest point with arms, hands and fingers extended. Do not wait to catch ball on its downward path. Change quickly from defense to offense, and score.

2. Run-the-Line Drill (Figure 6-1)

Purpose: To develop footwork, hip action, body balance and agility.

Procedure: Defender lines up in position, straddling a line, facing the coach, whom he will watch until the football is thrown or the latter signals end of drill (20 yards downfield). Using a crossover step, and reversing his feet as quickly as possible as he turns from side to side, the defender attempts to stay on the line. The objective is to run as fast as possible, yet make as many turns from side to side as possible, while looking straight ahead watching the passer (coach) the entire time. If ball is used, which is not necessary, defender plants, sprints to the interception point, and returns the football to the coach (passer). If ball is not used, coach signals end of drill, and defender turns around and starts down the line coming toward the coach but facing in the opposite direction. Manager can hand balls to coach.

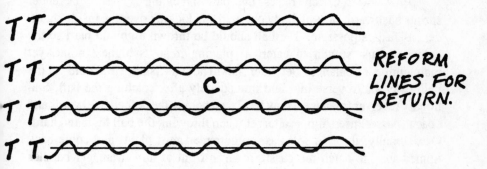

Figure 6-1

Coaching Points: Defender should *not* angle off the line as in (1) Defensive Wave Drill. Stress watching coach (passer) or looking straight ahead, and not watching the feet. Work up to an all-out effort, staying on the line, turning from side to side as quickly as possible and as many times as possible in the 40 yard distance.

3. Ball-Touch Drills

Purpose: To give defenders a feel for the types of passes they will come into contact with.

Procedure: This drill should be done 2 ways: (1) with defenders 15 yards away and facing the coach. When coach slaps ball the defender charges the coach, yelling "pass-pass-pass!" When the ball is in the air he yells "ball-ball-ball!" if he catches it he yells "Bingo!" Either way he returns the ball to the coach. He does not throw it back. (2) The defenders are 5 to 8 yards from the coach. When the coach slaps the ball they start back-pedaling, and follow with same communication calls. Coach should throw 4 groups of passes to all defenders: (A) Hard Pass, (B) Wobble Pass (end on end); (C) Bad Pass (high, low-wide); (D) Angle (Player breaks at 45° angle and coach throws ball. He must dive for it.)

Coaching Points: Watch for communication, hustle, and going after the ball aggressively with the hands.

4. Back-Up Interception Drill (Figure 6-2)

Purpose: To develop reaction, footwork, agility in going backward to catch the football.

Procedure: Coach raises the ball indicating "Pass." Defender sprints backward, turning body outward and looking over the inside shoulder, as fast as possible. The ball should be thrown high and hard so the defender must stretch to catch it, playing it at its highest point, yet maintaining his balance. Defender should not false-step. He should put the ball away and reverse his field immediately after catching the ball. Stationary receiver (manager) may be placed behind the defender 10 yards and coach (passer) uses him as a target when throwing the ball high and hard. Occasionally, throw a soft pass so defender must plant, and come back immediately to catch the pass thrown in front of him. Manager handles balls.

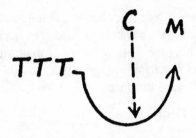

Figure 6-2

Coaching Points: Stress proper fundamentals of catching the football, putting it away, and running hard after intercepting the ball.

5. Forward-Backward-Diagonal Drill (Figure 6-3)

Purpose: To develop reaction, footwork, agility in changing direction in order to catch the football.

Procedure: Defender faces coach (passer) 6 to 8 yards apart, with two upright dummies half-way between them 2 to 3 yards apart. On signal, defender comes between the dummies with body under control, plants his foot and moves laterally several steps, breaking at a 90° angle until the coach raises the football as if to pass. Defender yells "Pass!," plants outside foot and sprints backward as fast as possible, yet watching the passer all the time. The ball may be thrown at any time he starts backward, as the drill is then like (4) Back-Up Interception Drill. Or coach may point left or right any time after the defender starts backward, and he must break on a diagonal angle for the ball which should be thrown immediately after pointing in the direction the defender should break. On intercepting the ball, the defender sounds off. Manager handles balls.

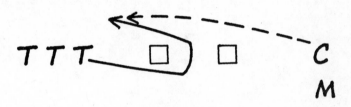

Figure 6-3

Coaching Points: Stress breaking at sharp angles, proper planting procedure. Defender does not move a great distance, as the emphasis should be on changing direction—forward, laterally, backward, diagonally. Conduct drill as follows. Stand with feet staggered. Pull ball to stomach indicating snap-back from center. Defender comes between dummies (3 to 4 steps) and has moved laterally (several steps). Raise ball behind ear (both hands on the football) simulating pass. Remove front hand, point, throw. Stress catching the ball properly.

6. Aggressive Interception Drills (Figure 6-4)

Purpose: To teach defender to concentrate on catching the ball, running through a receiver if necessary to intercept the ball when it is in the air.

Procedure: Upright dummy is placed between passer and defender. Ball is thrown so that defender must go through (over) dummy in order to make interception. Coach is the apex of an equilateral triangle 10 yards from defender and 10 yards from player holding an air bag. The latter two are 10 yards apart facing each other. As defender starts toward player with air bag, coach throws toward player holding shield (bag) timing-out pass so defender can intercept the ball as he approaches player holding air bag. Latter slams defender with shield after he makes interception. Defender should put the ball away immediately, lower his shoulder and use his body to ward off being slammed by the player with the air bag.

Figure 6-4

Coaching Points: Stress intercepting the pass and putting the ball away. Time-out passes properly in both phases of this drill. Stress playing the ball, ignoring opponent as defender goes for the interception.

7. Tip Interception Drills

a) Straight-Ahead Tip Drill.
b) Stationary (manager) Tip Drill.
c) Criss-Cross Tip Drill.
d) Side Tip Drill.

Purpose: To improve body control and reaction by getting the second man (trailer) to play the ball better by keeping his eyes on it.

Procedure: Same as (3) Ball-Touch Drill, only second man trails 5 yards behind the tipper, who runs three-quarters speed toward the passer in Straight-Ahead Tip Drill. A variation is for the manager to be stationed 7 yards in front of the coach (passer), facing him, with a football in his hands extended upward. The coach throws another football toward the one held by the manager, who deflects it backward into the air for the defender running toward him from behind to intercept. In Criss-Cross Tip Drill, the tipper crosses at an angle 7 yards in front of the coach (passer), and tips the ball back to the trailer crossing at an angle 5 yards behind him. In Side Tip Drill, the line of tippers moves from right to left parallel to the line of scrimmage 7 yards away from the coach, and the trailers move from left to right 5 yards behind them (in opposite direction). Reverse lines. Manager handles balls.

Coaching Points: Stress keeping the eyes on the ball, and catching it properly.

8. Combat Tip Drill (Figure 6-5)

Purpose: To develop competing for the deflected ball in flight.

Procedure: Same as Tip Drill, but two players approach the tipper and compete to intercept the deflected ball, simulating receiver and defender fighting to catch the football. Manager tips ball with another football and handles balls for coach.

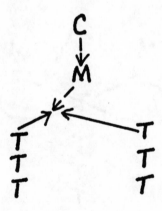

Figure 6-5

Coaching Points: Stress watching the ball, and not the opponent. Players may use body to ward off each other legally in attempting to catch the ball, but they should not push or shove illegally.

9. Defender's Leap Drill

Purpose: To develop leaping into the air to catch the football.

Procedure: Defenders (receivers), in a single column start on the 5-yard line and sprint toward the goal posts. First time through, defender (receiver) tries to touch the crossbar (10 feet from the ground) with his right hand; second time, left hand; and third time, both hands, simulating leaping into the air to catch or defend against the high pass.

Coaching Points: Stress gathering and leaping into the air without stopping, timing the take-off and touching the crossbar. Defender (receiver) should not grab the bar and/or attempt to swing on it. Also have players stand under the bar and attempt to jump from a stationary position and touch the crossbar. Good pre-practice drill as part of warm-up after players are loose.

10. Figure-8 Interception Drill (Figure 6-6)

Purpose: To develop catching the ball at various angles, and to give the interceptor maximum practice in catching the ball in a short period of time.

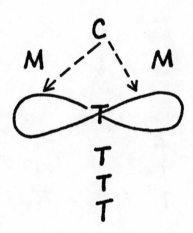

Figure 6-6

Procedure: Defender lines up 10 yards away from passer (coach) who has a manager on either side of him. Defender jogs through a Figure-8 pattern going back and forth toward each sideline in an area approximately 10 yards by 10 yards, and crossing at a point 10 yards in front of the coach each time. Passer throws the ball any time so that intercepter is taking it over either shoulder, coming to or going away from the passer. Defender tosses the ball to either manager after he catches it, or manager retrieves the ball if defender does not catch it.

Coaching Points: Actually a "Bad Pass Drill" for the defender. Emphasis is not on distance defender runs, but on catching the ball properly at various angles.

11. Reaction Drill (Figure 6-7)

Purpose: To develop reaction, body balance, proper position at all times, increase interception distance, and to play the ball in the air.

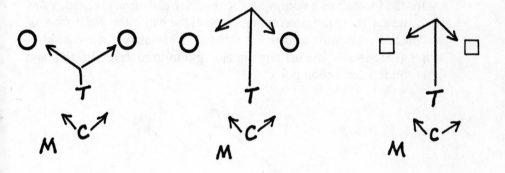

Figure 6-7

Procedure: Receivers are on both hash marks (or inside boundary on sideline and on one hash mark), and defender is in a good football position between them upfield and reads "Pass." He starts shuffling back faster and faster, watching the passer all the time. He does not favor either receiver as he is playing the field, and is going to sprint to intercept the ball, which will be thrown by the coach. (The coach will not fake; he will turn toward one receiver or the other.) If the ball is thrown in front of him, he sprints to it. If it is thrown behind and beyond him, he rolls back by turning his head and dropping far shoulder, getting depth as he sprints to catch the ball. The drill can be run with two bags in front of the receivers. The defender reacts to the ball, but does a hard tackle through the bag. Manager handles balls.

Coaching Points: Stress covering the field and playing the ball, not the receiver. At times throw deep, regardless of the depth of the receivers, so defender has to go all out to catch the ball. Build confidence by hanging ball in air, showing defender how much distance he can cover while sprinting to the interception point.

12. Roll-Back Drill (Figure 6-8)

Purpose: To teach playing football and intercepting the pass that is thrown beyond and behind the defender.

Procedure: Defenders set up in three-deep or two-deep (four-deep) positions. Start with the football in the middle of the field and move out to the hash marks. The passer should look at one of the defenders signaling him to go back to his area. The ball is thrown behind and beyond the defender or in front of him. In the former, the defender will roll back toward the football as he drops his far shoulder and turns his head, gains depth and sprints to the interception point. If the ball is thrown in front of the defender, the must change his direction immediately without false-stepping. He should use his arms in aiding him to reverse direction and sprint to the interception point.

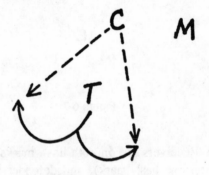

Figure 6-8

Coaching Points: Stress catching the football at the highest point possible, and not waiting to catch it on its downward descent. Check defender's steps after ball is thrown to determine how much ground is lost before he reacts forward toward the ball thrown in front of his position.

13. Position on Receiver Drill (Figure 6-9)

Purpose: To teach individual defender always to have proper position on the receiver.

Procedure: Defender sets up in a good defensive football position and reacts when coach raises arm indicating pass. Receiver runs a square-out pattern and passer (coach) places the ball so defender must go through the receiver in order to intercept the pass. At times, the ball should be thrown so defender can break past receiver and intercept the pass, in order to build confidence.

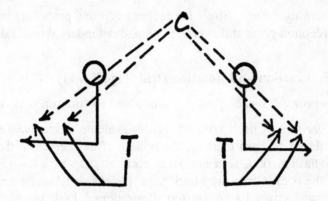

Figure 6-9

Coaching Points: Defender should maintain an approximate position of 3 yards vertically and 2 yards laterally outside the receiver until the ball is released. Check for false-stepping, and running in an arc. At times, underthrow and overthrow the receiver in order to determine if defender is playing the passer and the ball, or merely covering the receiver.

14. Overlap Drill (Figure 6-10)

Purpose: To teach and develop overlapping the flight of the football on a pass.

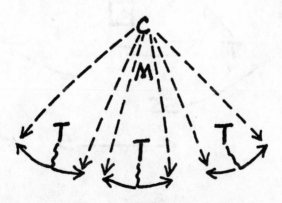

Figure 6-10

Procedure: Coach (passer) raises the football indicating pass, and defenders start shuffling back to cover their zones. Two defenders should be able to overlap the ball when it is thrown in the middle out to either halfback's position, and the halfback should be able to overlap the boundary when the ball is thrown outside of his position.

Coaching Points: Stress the proper angle and procedure in going to the interception point and overlapping, and defenders should talk to each other.

15. Reaction and Rotation Drill (Figure 6-11)

Purpose: To teach proper reaction and rotation on pass defense.

Procedure: Coach (passer) versus skeleton defensive secondary. Ball is placed on hash mark, in the middle of the field, and then on the opposite hash mark. Coach simulates receiving snap-back from center and goes to the pocket on a drop-back pass. Defensive secondary must react properly and cover its zones (top illustrations). Drill is repeated with quarterback (passer) rolling out, simulating a flow pass, and defenders (ends and linebackers added) react and rotate properly (bottom illustration). When coach (passer) stops running, all secondary defenders stop immediately so that he can check their positions with each other and to determine if they are getting width, depth and rotating properly. Emphasis is on maintaining proper field position in order to carry out responsibilities of coordinated pass defense.

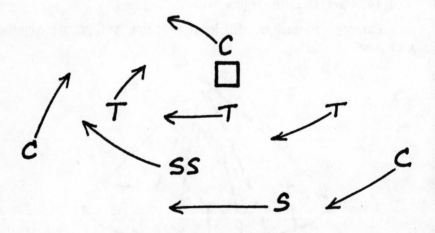

Figure 6-11

Coaching Points: Individual responsibilities, fundamentals and techniques of stance, position, and alignment are taught during the Individual Period, as defenders learn their proper alignment depends on field position, rotation, and coverage (top illustrations). They are then practiced during the Combination or Group Period (bottom illustration showing ends, linebackers and three-deep secondary versus flow pass), and scrimmaged during the Team Period. Stress coordinated pass defense, proper positions initially and proper angles in covering responsibilities (rotation). Drill precedes Skeleton Pass Defense-Offense Drill, which is also a Combination or Group Period drill, where offensive ends and backs are added as receivers, and defenders must read and react to keys properly. Move ball laterally every time from middle to hash marks.

16. Team Reaction Drill (Figure 6-12)

Purpose: To teach and develop coordinated pass defense, and to change quickly from defense to offense on a pass interception.

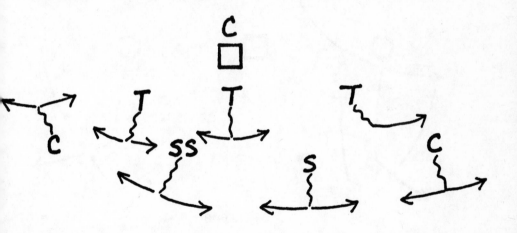

Figure 6-12

Procedure: Same as Tip only the ball is not deflected and as interceptor sounds off with interception signal teammates peel back or knock down the upright dummies which are stationed throughout the defensive secondary.

Coaching Points: Stress lining up quickly and accurately and taking proper paths to areas of responsibility. Stress scoring on the pass interception. Move from middle out to hash marks, and change defensive alignments.

17. 2-on-1 or Release Drill (Figure 6-13)

Purpose: To teach the defender to play his zone and the pass thrown in his zone properly.

Procedure: Defender is taught to play the deepest and widest receiver first, then the deepest, and to release when the ball is thrown and come up to cover the short receiver in his zone, if necessary. In the latter situation, defender releases from the deep man and either sprints to the interception point or "searches" the receiver, tackling him hard, forcing a fumble, if receiver already has caught the ball and defender cannot intercept or knock down the ball.

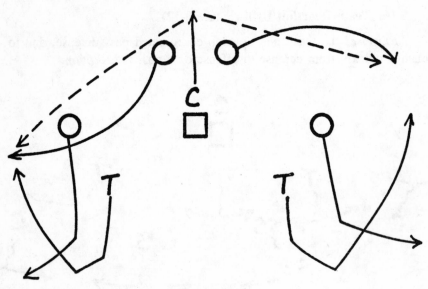

Figure 6-13

Coaching Points: Stress deep zone responsibility and not losing poise when passes are completed in front of the defender while he is covering deep. Passer should fake-pump short and throw long in order to determine if defender is playing the passer's arm motion, instead of the flight of the ball, and coming up quickly to cover the receiver nearest the line of scrimmage while permitting another receiver to get deep behind him. Change pass patterns, including the end running an out-pattern with the halfback going through, forcing the defender to release from the end and pick up the deep receiver. Check to see that defender plays the ball and zone and does not merely watch a single receiver. Build confidence that he can cover two men (or more) in his zone if he plays properly.

18. Back Pocket Coverage (Figure 6-14)

Purpose: To teach close, tight man-to-man coverage.

Procedure: Defender plays receiver as tight as possible with a hard inside shade. When the receiver moves off the line the defender gives him a good chug and forces him outside. The defender stays on the inside hip of the receiver, and when the receiver makes his move or looks for the ball, defender cuts in front of him and looks for the ball.

Figure 6-14

Coaching Points: Make sure the receiver never gets the inside break, find the ball quickly on break or find the receiver again if it hasn't been thrown yet. This is a goal line defensive tactic.

19. Man-to-Man Drill (Figure 6-15)

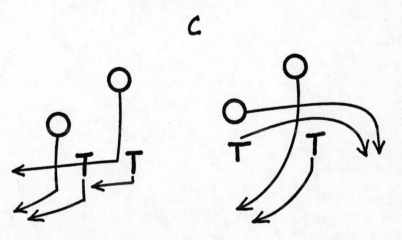

Figure 6-15

Purpose: To teach good man coverage.

Procedure: Put defender in normal position and mix up receivers' patterns.

Coaching Points: Defenders must have good foot action and body position. Don't let them turn their backs or cross their legs. Must keep cushion for 2 to 2.5 seconds. Play the receiver and the ball.

20. 7-on7 Drill: Do with linebackers exactly as discussed in linebacker chapter (Chapter 5).

Chapter 7

BREAKDOWN OF RULES, ASSIGNMENTS, COVERAGES, STUNTS AND TECHNIQUES TO BE USED WITH EVEN FRONTS

WE TAKE OUR BASIC FRONT (COLLEGE 4-3) and stay in it as much as possible. Our only adjustments are coverages and stunts unless a particular offensive formation forces a set adjustment. You can use this same philosophy with any of the even fronts discussed in this chapter. We don't believe in having a dozen different fronts and jumping from defense to defense. Our philosophy is to force and contain. We attempt to attack the offense on first down and force them to run a play which is inconsistent with their practice plans. An example of this would be to create a second-and-9 or longer. Most people spend very little time working on plays for this situation. We can then get into a defensive call that best suits the plays that we feel are available to them at that time.

The second aspect of our plan is containment. We strive never to give up the big play or long TD. It is our feeling that very few teams can put together drives of 60 or more yards. If you study the game closely, you will see that the good teams only do this about twice a game. Therefore, if we don't give up the big play and our offense doesn't create the big turnover we can control our destiny with this philosophy.

The following material is a breakdown of each of the even fronts that we feel are most successful in modern football. We have included all rules, coverages, stunts, and techniques necessary to run these defenses.

FACTORS PERTINENT TO THE DEFENSE

1. Names and Symbols of Defensive Personnel

Left defensive end	LE
Right defensive end	RE
Left defensive tackle	LT
Right defensive tackle	RT
Strong side linebacker (Sam)	S
Middle linebacker (Mike)	M
Weak side linebacker (Willie)	W
Weak side defensive cornerback	WC
Strong side defensive cornerback	SC
Strong side safety (Kat)	K
Weak side safety (Free safety)	F

2. Labeling of Defensive Gaps

To better define specific areas of defensive responsibility, each gap in the offensive line is lettered; from the nose of the center out, each letter designates a gap or area which extends to the head of the next offensive man. (Figure 7-1)

Figure 7-1

3. Defensive Alignments

For purposes of defining lateral alignments for the defense in relation to offensive linemen, we will use single digit numbers starting from inside to outside of offensive lineman. (Figure 7-2)

1. Your outside eye on the inside eye of offensive lineman.
2. Nose-to-nose with offensive lineman.
3. Your inside eye on the outside eye of offensive lineman.
4. Your inside shoulder on the outside shoulder of offensive lineman.

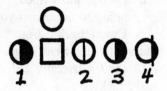

Figure 7-2

4. Defensive Huddle

Structure: Our huddle will be a 2-line formation huddle, facing the defensive quarterback and ball. Front line aligns toe-to-toe and second line shoulder-to-shoulder. (Figure 7-3)

Procedure: Left tackle is responsible for calling "huddle" 1 yard from the ball. Defensive quarterback will stand facing the defensive huddle. He will call "set." Front line will shift to hands on knees. All eyes focus on signal caller and maintain strict silence. Signal caller will make defensive call twice, then break huddle by command of "ready" and entire defensive unit will clap hands and break huddle.

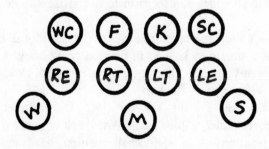

Figure 7-3

5. Definitions of Terminology Pertinent to Defense

1. L.O.S.—Line of scrimmage
2. P.O.A.—Point of attack
3. Front—Refers to defensive ends, tackles, and linebackers
4. Perimeter—Refers to corners, Kat and safety
5. Strong side—Tight end side of formation
6. Weak side—Side of formation without tight end
7. Near back—The running back nearest you
8. Drop-back pass—Quarterback drops back approximately straight back in area between offensive guards and sets up to pass
9. Pull-up pass—QB moves laterally before setting up to pass inside his offensive tackles
10. Sprint-out pass—QB moves laterally outside his offensive tackle before passing or running
11. Play Action pass—Offensive maneuver where a pass is thrown after faking run action
12. Throwback pass—Offensive maneuver where QB moves in one direction and passes back in the opposite direction
13. Motion—Extended movement by an offensive back prior to the snap of the ball
14. Pursuit—Movement to the ball, after initial defensive responsibility has been fulfilled, at the proper angle
15. Gang Tackling—Maximum pursuit by the entire defensive unit in order to make contact on ball carrier
16. Hand Shiver—A defensive technique in which a blow is delivered with the heels of the hands by extending the arms and locking the elbows on contact; used to keep blockers away from body and legs
17. Forearm shiver—Aggressive, punishing defensive technique using the shoulder and forearm to neutralize and destroy high blocks
18. Skate—A shuffling technique where outside foot is kept back, shoulders square to L.O.S. to prevent being hooked
19. Quick receiver—Any eligible pass receiver on or close to L.O.S. (ends, wing, slot or flankers)
20. ARC Release—By the T.E. or slot, receiver releases in an outside arc either to block defensive back or run a pass route
21. Eagle position—A good football position, head and eyes up, back arched, tail low, legs spread comfortably for balance, weight on balls of feet, arms hanging loosely in front of body;

from this hit position, you are ready to deliver and to react quickly in any direction

22. Option Responsibilities—

    #1—Indicates running back plunging into the line

    #2—Indicates quarterback

    #3—Indicates running back to whom the quarterback may pitch the ball

23. Neutral Zone—The space between the offense and defense—the length of the ball

24. Front side—The side to which the play is directed

25. Back side—The side away from which the play is directed

26. Lead step—To step first with foot toward the direction in which you are going

27. Crossover step—To step first with the back side foot

28. Penetrate—Charge taken by defensive man to get into offensive backfield

29. Unbalanced Line—A set where 4 offensive linemen are on one side of center

30. Wingback—A back who takes his position 1 yard behind the L.O.S. and 3 yards or less outside the tight end

31. Slotback—A back who takes his position 1 yard behind the L.O.S. and between the split end and tackle

32. Flanker—A back who takes his position 1 yard behind the L.O.S. and 3 yards or more outside the tight end

33. Split end—An end who splits 5 yards or more outside the tackle

34. Spread—2 quick receivers to each side

35. Trips—3 quick receivers to one side

36. Trap—A play where a defensive player is drawn across L.O.S.

37. Draw—A play where a pass is faked. The offensive linemen pass block the lineman to the outside, enabling the ball carrier to break between the rushing linemen

38. Flex—A split taken by the tight end between 2 and 5 yards from the tackle

39. Hip—Position taken by Willie, 1 yard deep and 1 yard outside the outside leg of the defensive end

40. Drive block—Lineman's head fires straight at you; will block you either way

41. Down block—Lineman blocks to your inside on next defender

42. Scoop block—Lineman reaches to play side area, picking up any opposite jersey that shows in that area

43. Turn-out—Lineman's head goes inside trying to turn out the defensive man
44. Turn in—Lineman's head goes outside trying to turn in the defensive man
45. Quick block—Used on quick passes. Line fires out trying to get defensive hands down
46. Hook block—Aggressive block by the offense when their head goes to the outside and the lineman tries to seal the defender inside
47. Cross block—Change in assignments between 2 linemen
48. Crack-back block—Maneuver where a wide receiver angles sharply to the inside block
49. Log block—Pulling lineman tries to seal defender inside
50. Double team—Inside lineman drive blocks defender and outside lineman attacks defender from side
51. Cloud—Call for corner back support in flat or run support
52. Sky—Call for Kat or safety support in flat or run support
53. SAG—Strong side tackle aligns 1 yard off the L.O.S.
54. WAG—Weak side tackle aligns 1 yard off the L.O.S.
55. BAG—Both tackles align 1 yard off the L.O.S.
56. Walk away—Alignment by Willie, splitting the split end and the defensive end
57. Hold up—Alignment by Willie on split end, forcing an outside release
58. O.T.L. on the line, run it again—repeat play

6. Offensive Formations (Figure 7-4)

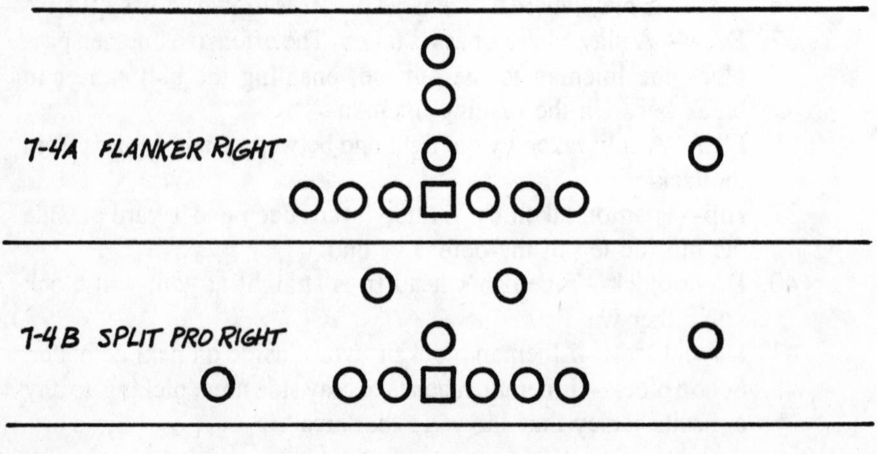

7-4A FLANKER RIGHT

7-4B SPLIT PRO RIGHT

Figure 7-4

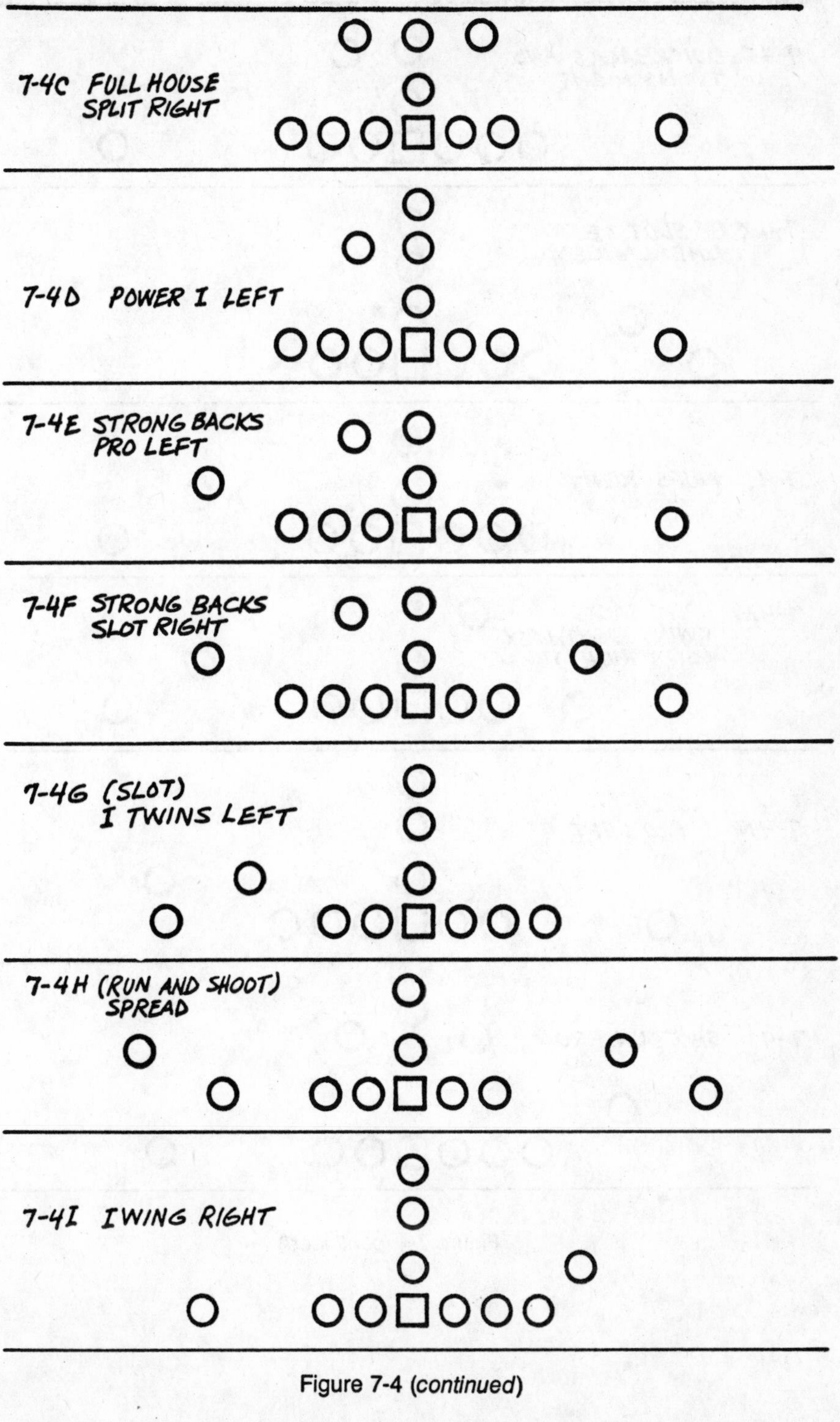

7-4C FULL HOUSE
SPLIT RIGHT

7-4D POWER I LEFT

7-4E STRONG BACKS
PRO LEFT

7-4F STRONG BACKS
SLOT RIGHT

7-4G (SLOT)
I TWINS LEFT

7-4H (RUN AND SHOOT)
SPREAD

7-4I I WING RIGHT

Figure 7-4 (continued)

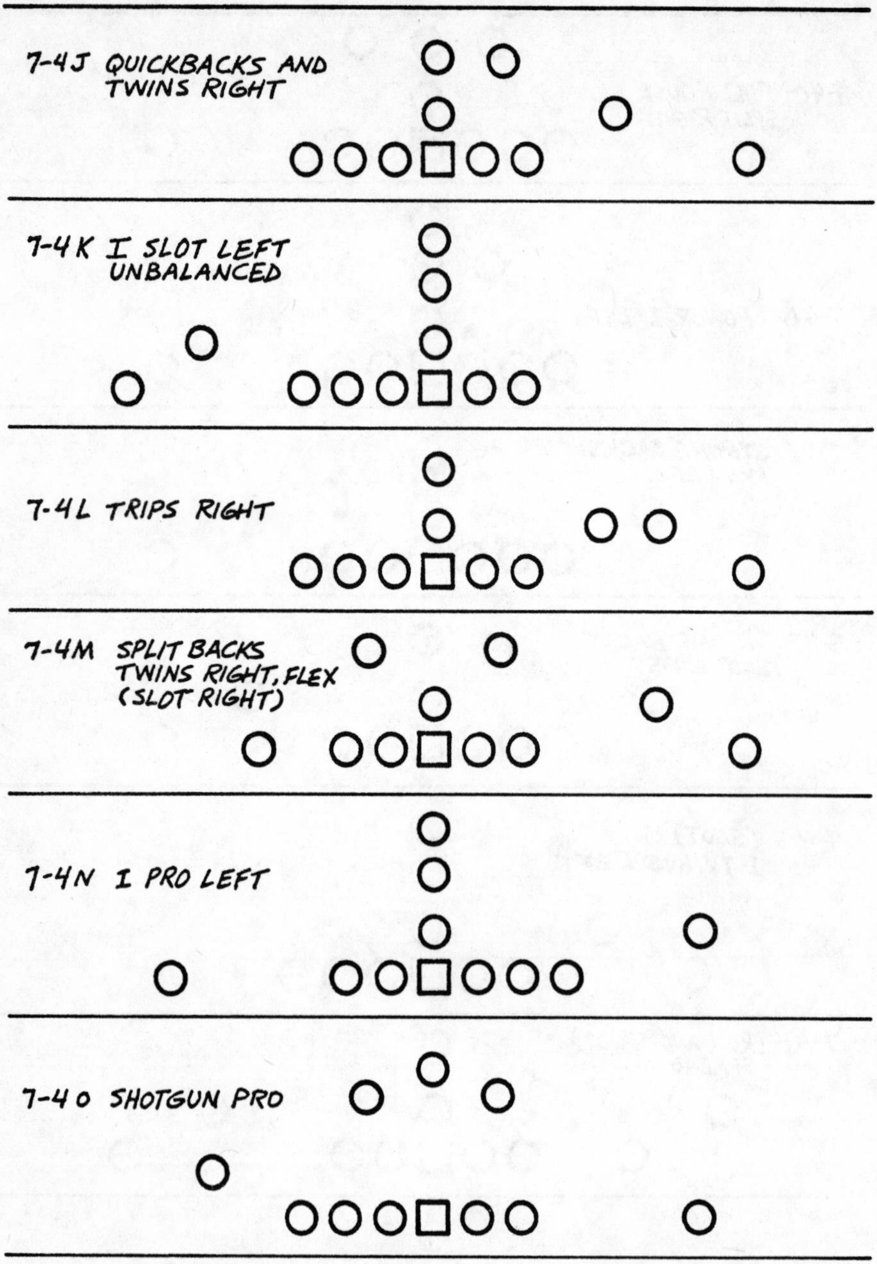

7-4J QUICKBACKS AND
　　　TWINS RIGHT

7-4K I SLOT LEFT
　　　UNBALANCED

7-4L TRIPS RIGHT

7-4M SPLIT BACKS
　　　TWINS RIGHT, FLEX
　　　(SLOT RIGHT)

7-4N I PRO LEFT

7-4O SHOTGUN PRO

Figure 7-4 *(continued)*

7. Numbering of Receivers (Figure 7-5)

   A. Widest receiver from center to either side is #1.
   B. Second widest from center receiver to either side is #2.
   C. Third widest from center receiver is #3.
   D. In the I formation first back who comes to the strong side is #3. First back to weak side is #2. Both backs come strong. First man in pattern is #3. Both backs come weak, first man in pattern is #2.

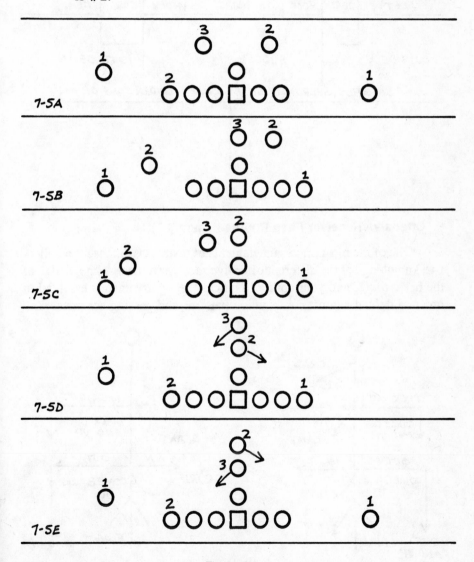

Figure 7-5

8. Pass Zones (Figure 7-6)

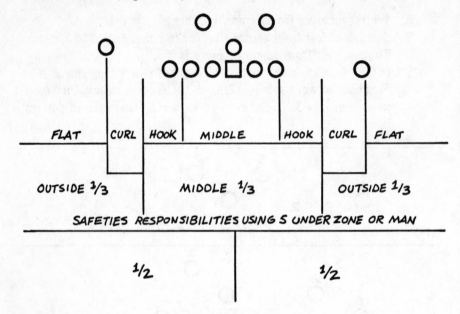

Figure 7-6

9. Offensive Receiver Pass Routes (Figure 7-7)

One of the most important elements of team pass defense is a collective knowledge of the different offensive receiver routes. A knowledge of the basic routes and your ability to quickly recognize each is essential in order to defend against combination patterns and passing schemes.

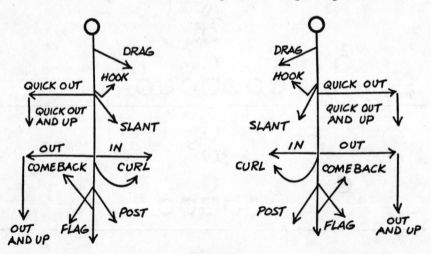

Figure 7-7

Backs Possible Flare Control (Figure 7-8)

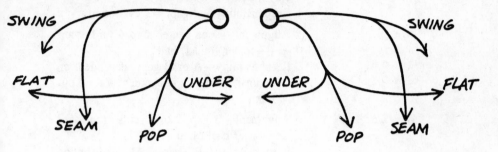

Figure 7-8

40 (Figure 7-9)

Our basic front will be used in all situations with any of our stunts or coverages. All defenses draw against strong left set or tight end left.

Figure 7-9

Strong End:	Alignment—3 on tight end Key—tight end's head Responsibility—D area, #2 vs. option
Weak End:	Alignment—inside shoulder on offensive tackle's outside shoulder (4 alignment) Key—tackle's head Responsibility—C area, #2 vs. option
Strong Tackle:	Alignment—2 on the guard Key—guard's head Responsibility—strong A or B gap, dependent on defensive call. #1 vs. option
Weak Tackle:	Alignment—2 on the guard Key—guard's head Responsibility—weak A or B gap, dependent on defensive call. #1 vs. option

SAM: Alignment—3 on the tackle, 2 to 4 yards deep
                        Key—tackle's head
                        Responsibility—C gap, #1 vs. option

MIKE: Alignment—O on center, 2 to 4 yards deep
                        Key—center's head, ball
                        Responsibility—A or B gaps, dependent on
                            defensive tackle's assignment #1 vs. op-
                            tion

WILLIE: Alignment—B gap, 2 to 4 yards deep
                        Key—near back, ball
                        Responsibility—B gap, #1 vs. option
                            (change up an option, #3 vs. option)

*We must give inside/outside assignment to strong side end. SAM will take opposite responsibility.

$$\text{End} \begin{cases} \text{Inside} = \text{Run} \\ \text{Outside} = \text{Pass} \end{cases}$$

40 Over (Figure 7-10)

Over-shifted defensive front not to be used vs. 2 tight ends. Will be used with our stunts and any coverages.

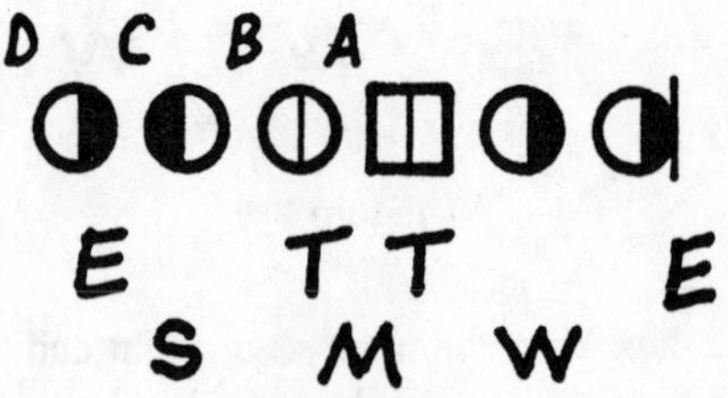

Figure 7-10

Strong End: Alignment—3 on tight end
                        Key—tight end's head
                        Responsibility—D area, #2 vs. option

Weak End: Alignment—inside shoulder on offensive
                            tackle's outside shoulder (4 alignment)
                        Key—tackle's head
                        Responsibility—C area, #2 vs. option

Strong Tackle: Alignment—2 on guard
                        Key—guard's head
                        Responsibility—A or B gap, dependent on
                            defensive call. #1 vs. option

Weak Tackle:	Alignment—2 on center
	Key—center's head
	Responsibility—either A gap, dependent on defensive call #1 vs. option
SAM:	Alignment—3 on tackle, 2 to 4 yards deep
	Key—tackle's head, ball
	Responsibility—C gap #1 vs. option
MIKE:	Alignment—A gap 2 to 4 yards deep
	Key—ball
	Responsibility—dependent on defensive tackle's assignment #1 vs. option
WILLIE:	Alignment—3 on guard, 2 to 4 yards deep
	Key—guard's head, ball
	Responsibility—B gap, #1 vs. option (change up an option, #3 vs. option)

*We must give inside/outside assignment to strong side end. SAM will take opposite responsibility.

Inside = Run
Outside = Pass

50 (Figure 7-11)

A fundamental defensive front. May be used with all stunts and coverages.

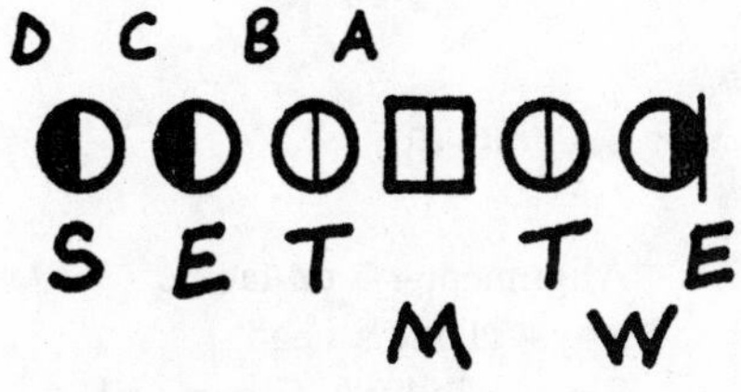

Figure 7-11

Strong End:	Alignment—3 on tackle
	Key—tackle's head
	Responsibility—C gap, #1 vs. option
Weak End:	Alignment—inside shoulder on offensive tackle's outside shoulder (4 alignment)
	Key—tackle's head
	Responsibility—C area, #2 vs. option

Strong Tackle:	Alignment—2 on guard Key—guard's head Responsibility—strong A or B gap, dependent on defensive call, #1 vs. option
SAM:	Alignment—3 on tight end Key—tight end's head, ball Responsibility—D area, #2 vs. option
MIKE:	Alignment—2 on center 2 to 4 yards deep Key—center's head, ball Responsibility—A or B gaps, dependent on defensive tackle's assignment #1 vs. option
WILLIE:	Alignment—B gap, 2 to 4 yards deep Key—near back, ball Responsibility—B gap, #1 vs. option (Change up vs. option#3)

50 Over (Figure 7-12)

Over-shifted front to be used vs. teams who run the ball to the tight end side, not to be used vs. 2 tight ends.

Figure 7-12

Strong End:	Alignment—3 on tackle Key—tackle's head Responsibility—C gap, #1 vs. option
Weak End:	Alignment—inside shoulder on offensive tackle's outside shoulder (4 alignment) Key—tackle's head Responsibility—C area, #2 vs. option
Strong Tackle:	Alignment—2 on the guard Key—guard's head Responsibility—strong A or B gap, dependent on defensive call, #1 vs. option

Weak Tackle:	Alignment—2 on the center
	Key—center's head
	Responsibility—either A gap, dependent on defensive call, #1 vs. option
SAM:	Alignment—3 on tight end's head
	Key—tight end's head, ball
	Responsibility—D area, #2 vs. option
MIKE:	Alignment—strong A gap, 2 to 4 yards deep
	Key—Ball
	Responsibility—dependent on defensive tackle's assignment
WILLIE:	Alignment—3 on guard, 2 to 4 yards deep
	Key—guard's head, ball
	Responsibility—weak B gap, #1 vs. option

44 (Figure 7-13)

This is an eight-man front using a three-deep secondary. Excellent stunting and blitzing defense, with linebackers in good position for pass drops and pursuit.

Figure 7-13

Strong End:	Alignment—3 point stance, 2 on tight end
	Key—tight end's head
	Responsibility—D area, #2 vs. option
Weak End:	Alignment—3-point stance, 1 yard outside offensive tackle
	Key—offensive tackle, near back
	Responsibility—C area, #2 vs. option
Strong Tackle:	Alignment—3- or 4-point stance, 2 on guard
	Key—guard's head
	Responsibility—strong A or B gap, dependent on defensive call, #1 vs. option

Weak Tackle:	Alignment—3- or 4-point stance, 2 on guard Key—guard's head Responsibility—weak A or B gap, dependent on defensive call, #1 vs. option
SAM:	Alignment—2 on tight end, 2-4 yards deep Key—near back through offensive tackle Responsibility—C gap, #3 vs. option
Strong MIKE:	Alignment—2 on strong guard, 2-4 yards deep Key—near back Responsibility—strong A or B gap, dependent on defensive tackle's assignment, #1 vs. option
Weak MIKE:	Alignment—2 on weak guard, 2-4 yards deep Key—near back Responsibility—weak A or B gap, dependent on defensive tackle's assignment, #1 vs. option
WILLIE:	Alignment—depending on situation, will use hip, walk away or hold up alignment Key—near back or split end Responsibility—D area, #3 vs. option

4-4 over adjustment—only versus 1 tight end and teams that run to tight end side.

60 Split (Figure 7-14)

This is an eight-man front using a three-deep secondary, very strong inside vs. the run and an excellent pursuing and containing defense.

Figure 7-14

Strong End:	Alignment—2-point stance, 1-2 yards outside the tight end, depending on the situation Key—tight end and near back Responsibility—D area, #2 vs. option
Weak End:	Alignment—depending on situation, will use hip, walk away or hold-up alignment Key—near back or split end Responsibility—D area, #3 vs. option
Strong Tackle:	Alignment—3-point stance, 1 on tight end Key—tight end's head Responsibility—C gap, #1 vs. option
Weak Tackle:	Alignment—3-point stance, 1 yard outside the offensive tackle Key—near back Responsibility—C area, #2 vs. option
Strong Guard:	Alignment—3- or 4-point stance, 3 on guard Key—guard's head Responsibility—strong A or B gap, dependent on defensive call, #1 vs. option
Weak Guard:	Alignment—3- or 4-point stance, 3 on guard Key—guard's head Responsibility—weak A or B gap, dependent on defensive call, #1 vs. option
Strong MIKE:	Alignment—A gap, shaded inside or outside depending on situation, 1-3 yards deep Key—center and QB Responsibility—strong A or B gap, dependent on defensive guard's assignment, #1 vs. option
Weak MIKE:	Alignment—A gap, shaded inside or outside depending on situation, 1-3 yards deep Key—center and QB Responsibility—weak A or B gap, dependent on defensive guard's assignment, #1 vs. option

60 Wide (Figure 7-15)

This is an eight-man front using a three-deep secondary. Very strong against the run, particularly versus the outside running game and the option game.

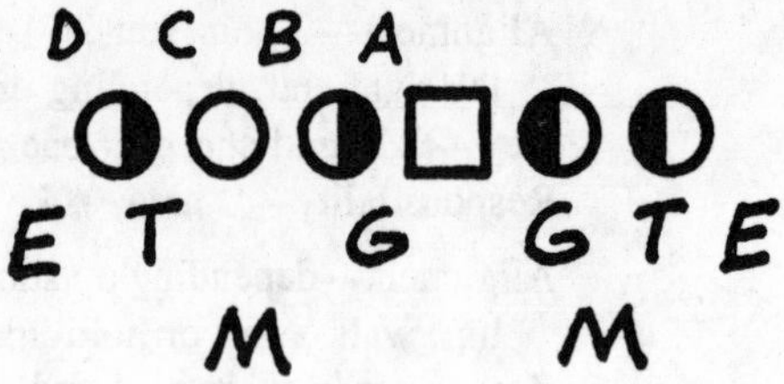

D C B A

O O O □ O O

E T G G T E

M   M

Figure 7-15

Strong End:	Alignment—2-point stance, 1-2 yards outside the tight end, depending on the situation Key—tight end and near back Responsibility—D area, #2 vs. option
Weak End:	Alignment—depending on situation, will use hip, walk away or hold-up alignment Key—near back or split end Responsibility—D area, #3 vs. option
Strong Tackle:	Alignment—3-point stance, 1 on tight end Key—tight end's head Responsibility—C gap, #1 vs. option
Weak Tackle:	Alignment—3-point stance, 1 yard outside the offensive tackle Key—near back or split end Responsibility—D area, #3 vs. option
Strong Guard:	Alignment—3- or 4-point stance, 2 on the guard Key—guard's head Responsibility—strong A or B gap, dependent on defensive call, #1 vs. option
Weak Guard:	Alignment—3- or 4-point stance, 2 on the guard Key—guard's head Responsibility—weak A or B gap, dependent on defensive call, #1 vs. option
Strong MIKE:	Alignment—2 on tackle, 2-4 yards deep Key—tackle's head, near back Responsibility—strong A or B gap, dependent on defensive guard's assignment, #1 vs. option

Weak MIKE:	Alignment—2 on tackle, 2-4 yards deep
	Key—tackle's head, near back
	Responsibility—weak A or B gap, dependent on defensive guard's assignment, #1 vs. option

65 (Figure 7-16)

Penetrating defense which we will use inside our 6-yard line. May be used up-field in short yardage situations. We will use our stunts and man coverage. Personnel change needed for 60 front.

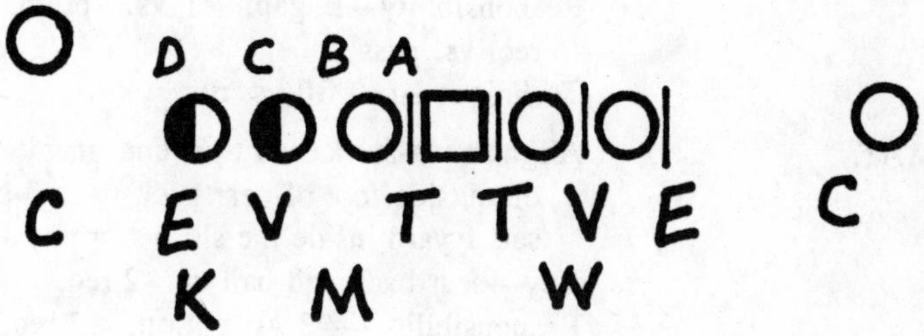

O D C B A
O O O|O|□|O|O| O
C E V T T V E   C
   K M   W

Figure 7-16

Tackles:	Alignment—in the A gap, crowding the football (inside 2-yard line—go shoulder-to-shoulder with center)
	Key—ball
	Responsibility—A gap, #1 vs. option
	Technique—4-point attacking stance, penetrate and attack the ball. Get to depth of QB's heels
Victors:	Alignment—3 on tackle, crowding the football
	Key—tackle's head
	Responsibility—C gap, #1 vs. option
	Technique—aggressive charge, penetrate and attack the ball
Ends:	Alignment—3 on tight end
	Key—tight end's head
	Responsibility—D area, #2 vs. option— slam technique, containing rush vs. pass
	Technique—aggressive control of tight end

MIKE:	Alignment—2 on center vs. balanced set 3 on guard vs. I set, inside foot on outside foot of near back vs. all other sets Key—near back and ball Responsibility—B gap, #1 vs. option, #3 rec. vs. pass Technique—fast fill vs. run
WILLIE:	Alignment—3 on guard vs. I set, inside foot on outside foot of near back vs. all other sets Key—near back and ball Responsibility—B gap, #1 vs. option, #2 rec. vs. pass Technique—fast fill vs. run
KAT:	Alignment—stack over tight end, inside foot on outside foot of near back vs. a 3-back set; 1 yard inside the slot vs. a twins set Key—near back and ball or #2 rec. Responsibility—#3 vs. option, #2 rec. vs. pass Technique—fast fill vs. run
Corners:	Alignment—1 yard outside nose of #1 rec. split less than 2 yards; 1 yard inside nose of #1 rec. split more than 2 yards. Vertical—½ distance to goal line Key—#1 receiver Responsibility—# vs. option, #1 rec. vs. pass Technique—tight man coverage

*vs. a split end set, the Victor on the split end side should slide to the B gap and play aggressive, penetrating football from there.

65 Over (Figure 7-17)

A penetrating, over-shifted goal line and short yardage defense. We will use our stunts and man coverage. Not to be used vs. 2-tight end offenses. Personnel change needed for 60 front.

Strong Tackle:	Alignment—2 on guard Key—ball

Responsibility—A or B gap, dependent on
defense called, #1 vs. option
Technique—attack

O D C B A
O O O O O O O   O
C E V T T V E   C
K M W

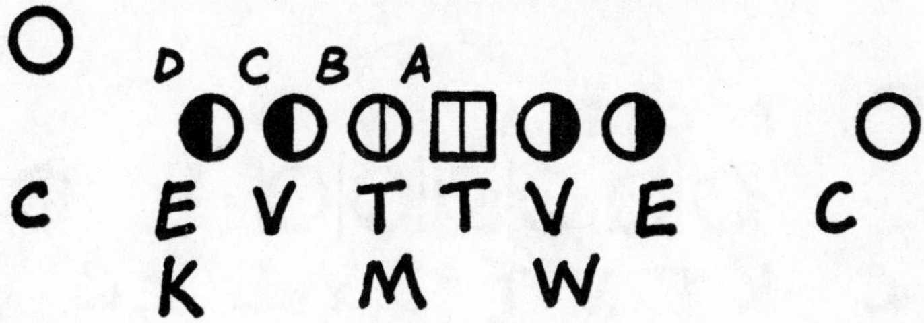

Figure 7-17

Weak Tackle: Alignment—2 on center
Key—ball
Responsibility—either A gap, dependent on
defense called, #1 vs. option
Technique—attack

Strong Victor: Alignment—3 on tackle
Key—tackle's head
Responsibility—B gap, #1 vs. option
Technique—same as 60

Weak Victor: Alignment—3 on guard
Key—guard's head
Responsibility—B gap, #1 vs. option
Technique—same as 60

Strong End: Alignment—3 on tight end
Key—tight end's head
Responsibility—D area, #2 vs. option, con-
taining rush vs. pass
Technique—same as 60

Weak End: Alignment—3 on tackle
Key—tackle's head
Responsibility—C area, #2 vs. option, con-
taining rush vs. pass
Technique—same as 60

MIKE: Same as 60

WILLIE: Same as 60

KAT: Same as 60

Corners: Same as 60

65 Squeeze (Figure 7-18)

A penetrating defense which will be used in very short yardage situations. We will use man coverage. Personnel change needed for 60 front.

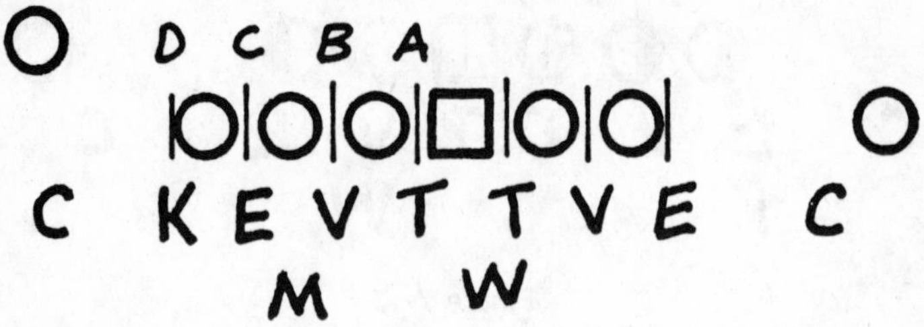

Figure 7-18

Tackles: Alignment—shoulder-to-shoulder with center, crowding the L.O.S.
Key—ball
Responsibility—A gap, #1 vs. option, stop the QB sneak
Technique—4-point, attacking stance.
Penetrate and attack the center, stopping the sneak. Stay low. Get to depth of QB's heels.

Victors: Alignment—B gap, crowding the L.O.S.
Key—ball
Responsibility—B gap, #1 vs. option
Technique—4-point, attacking stance.
Penetrate and attack the gap. Stay low.

Ends: Alignment—A on tight end side. Use 3- or 4-point stance in C gap, crowding the L.O.S. B on split end side use 2-point stance
Key—tackle's head
Responsibility—C gap, containing rush vs. pass
Technique—A on tight end side, aggressive penetrating charge through the C gap. #1 vs. option. B on split end side, aggressive charge outside of tackle. #2 vs. option

MIKE:	Alignment—same as 60
	Key—same as 60
	Responsibility—free flow to the ball
	Technique—fast fill vs. run
WILLIE:	Alignment—same as 60
	Key—same as 60
	Responsibility—free flow to the ball
	Technique—fast fill vs. run
Corner vs. Split end or Flanker:	Alignment—same as 60
	Key—same as 60
	Responsibility—same as 60
	Technique—same as 60
Corner and KAT vs. Tight End:	Alignment—3 alignment on tight end
	Key—tight end's head
	Responsibility—D area vs. run, #2 vs. option, Slam Tech., #2 vs. pass
	Technique—A vs. pass—hold up tight end and play tight man coverage. B vs. run—read tight end's block. Be aggressive, attack and penetrate, make something happen.

Attack (Figure 7-19)

1. This is a penetrating stunt involving the tackles, using a lead step and arm whip to protect trail leg.
2. Assignments will vary depending on front and direction of the attack.
3. Attack will be strong, weak, in or out.
4. We never will run attack in from 40 over, 50 over, or 44 over.
5. Assignments will vary for LBs, according to call for the tackles. It will be the strong B gap, strong A gap, weak A gap, or weak B gap

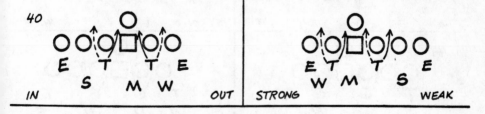

Figure 7-19

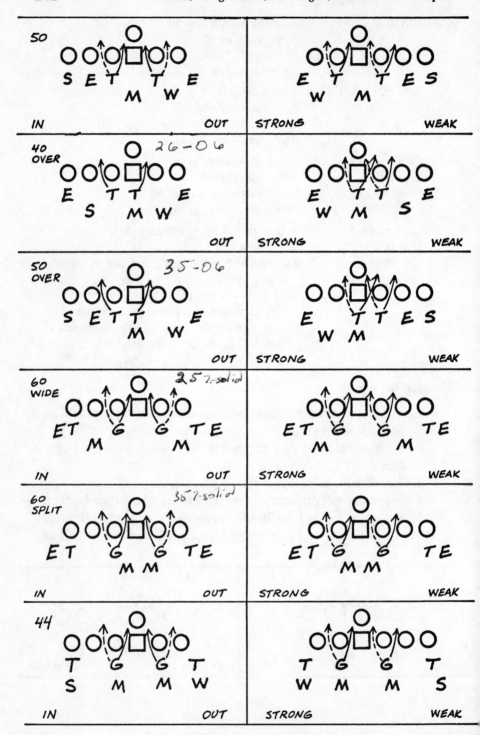

Figure 7-19 *(continued)*

Pinch (Figure 7-20)

1. This is a penetrating stunt involving the linemen penetrating their inside gaps.
2. Used mainly in short yardage situations.
3. Will be called strong side, weak side, or double.
4. Never double-pinch from 40 over, 50 over or 44 over.

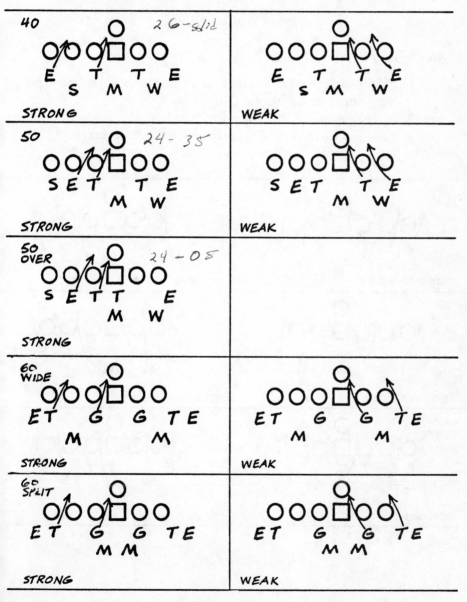

Figure 7-20

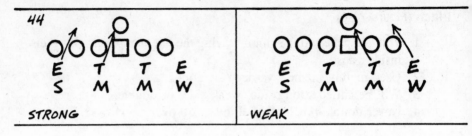

Figure 7-20 (*continued*)

Go (Figure 7-21)

1. This is an aggressive, attacking stunt used in short yardage to get maximum pressure on the QB.
2. Assignments will vary upon front used.
3. Must use Cover V or Cover V—no free pass coverage.

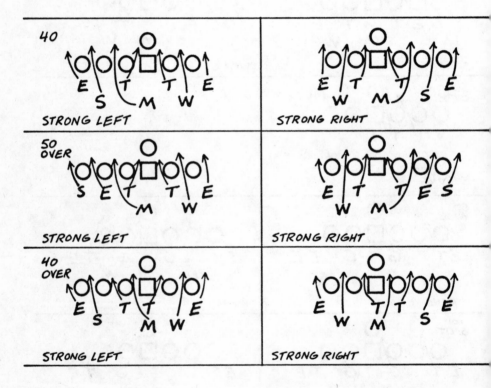

Figure 7-21

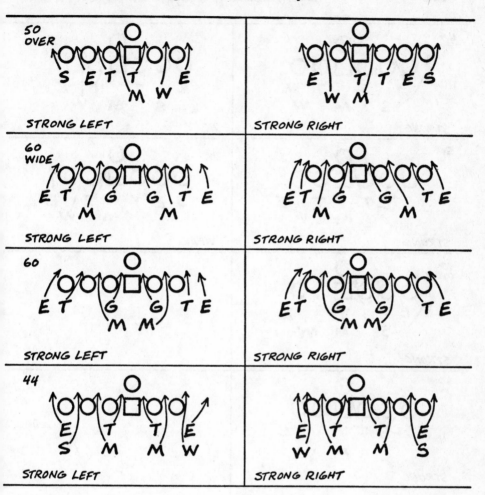

Figure 7-21 (*continued*)

Twist (Figure 7-22)

1. This is a penetrating stunt with the end and outside linebacker involved in the stunt crossing and switching assignments, with the tackle attacking inside.
2. Assignments will vary, depending on the front used.
3. Stunt will be run strong side, weak side or both sides.
4. Never double-twist from 40 over, 50 over or 44 over.

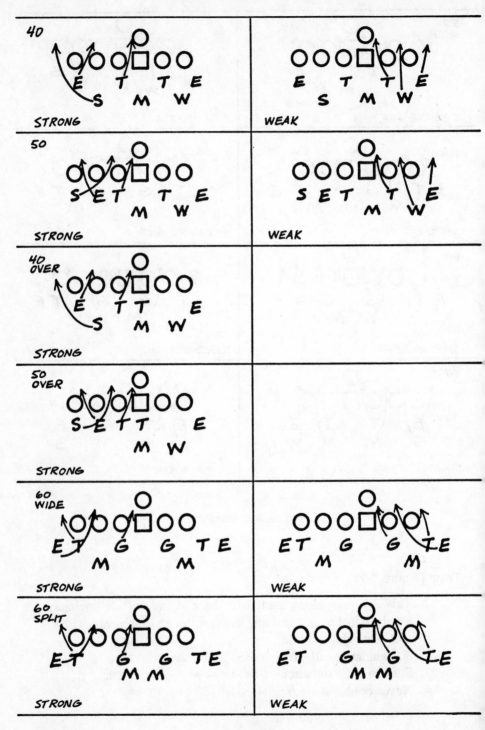

Figure 7-22

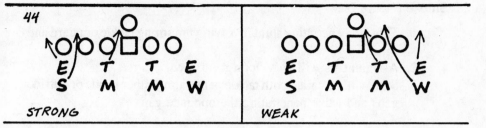

Figure 7-22 *(continued)*

Switch (Figure 7-23)

1. This is a penetrating stunt where the end and tackle cross and switch assignments.
2. Assignments will vary depending on front.
3. A. Sag—strong side tackle set 1 yard off the ball.
   B. Wag—weak side tackle set 1 yard off the ball.
   C. Bag—both tackles set 1 yard off the ball.

From the Sag, Wag, or Bag the tackles will be in a better position to execute the switch stunt.

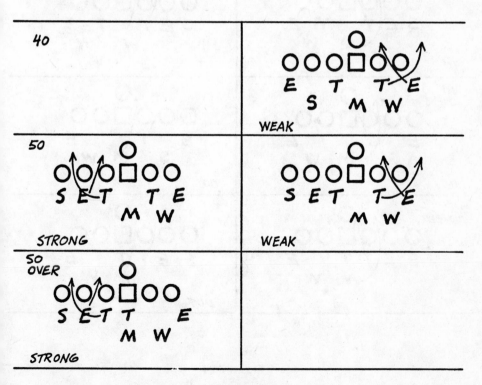

Figure 7-23

Smoke (Figure 7-24)

   1. This is a penetrating stunt involving the strong tackle or guard and Mike.
   2. Assignments will vary upon front used.
   3. Stunt will be called with tackle penetrating either inside or outside gaps and Mike penetrating the opposite gap.

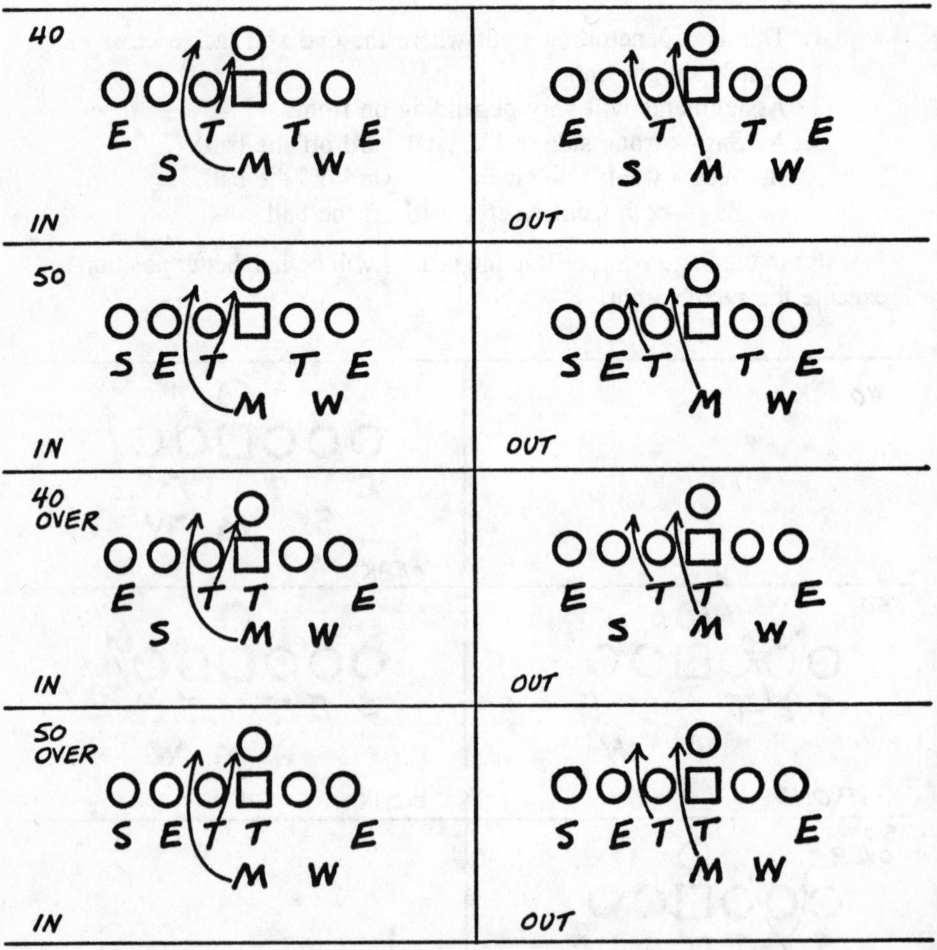

Figure 7-24

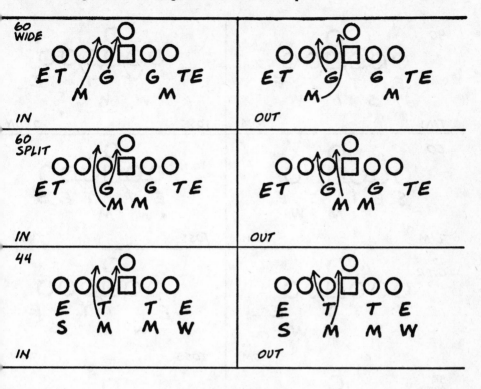

Figure 7-24 (*continued*)

Read (Figure 7-25)

1. Tackles will never be expected to control both sides of an offensive lineman. The side you are to control will be indicated as such:

   a. Tom—Both tackles will control the *outside* of the linemen they align on.

   b. Tim—Both tackles will control the *inside* of the linemen they align on.

   c. Toss—Both tackles will control the *strong side* of the linemen they align on.

   d. Twin—Both tackles will control the *weak side* of the linemen they align on.

2. This is a reading, non-penetrating stunt.

3. Assignments will vary for LBs, according to call for the tackles. It will be the strong B gap, strong A gap, weak A gap, or weak B gap.

4. Never Tim from 40 over, 50 over, or 44 over.

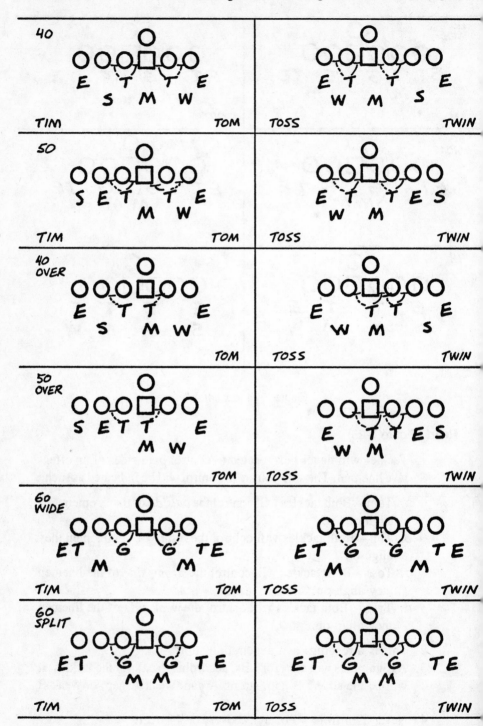

Figure 7-25

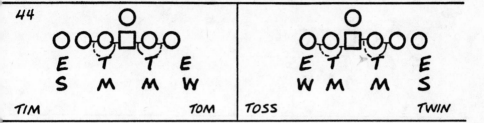

Figure 7-25 *(continued)*

Blood (Figure 7-26)

1. This is a penetrating stunt by the strong side, weak side, or both sides.
2. Used in short yardage situations.
3. Assignments will vary according to front used.
4. Never double-blood from 40 over, 50 over, or 44 over.

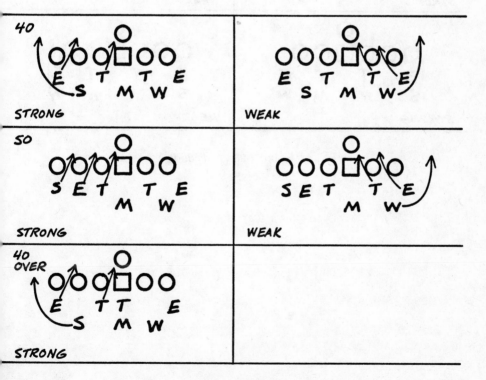

Figure 7-26

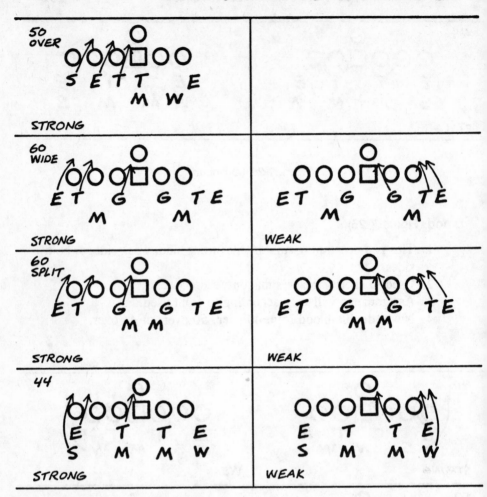

Figure 7-26 (continued)

Cover I (Figure 7-27)

Cover I is a zone coverage with rotation based on ball direction. We want to guarantee a sky force to the strong side. On the weak side, we will call our force according to formation. We will not rotate to the weak side.

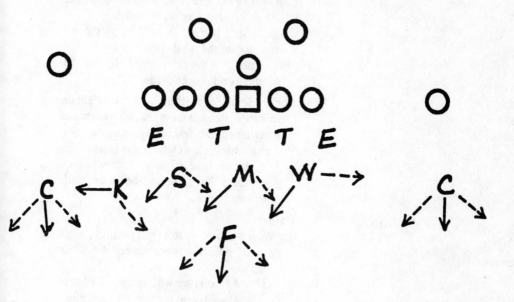

Figure 7-27

CALLS:

Cloud—	Call made by Kat or safety to corner, indicating corner has force on run toward him. On pass he has flat if ball comes toward him or it is a pocket pass and he is the strong corner. Kat or safety will have secondary force on run toward him. On pass toward him Kat or safety has deep outside 1/3 zone. On pass away Kat or safety has middle 1/3 zone. On pocket pass Kat will have deep outside 1/3 and safety will have middle 1/3 zone.
Sky—	Call made by Kat or safety to corner, indicating corner has secondary force on run toward him. On any type of pass he has deep outside 1/3 zone. Kat or safety will

have force on run toward them. On pass toward him Kat or safety has the flat. On pass away Kat or safety has middle 1/3 zone. On pocket pass Kat has flat and safety has middle 1/3.

Call will be *sky* to strong side unless split of #1 receiver is *less* than *5 yards*.
Cloud if split is *8 yards* or *less*, by the #1 receiver on the weak side.
Sky if split is *8 yards* or *more*, by the #1 receiver on the weak side.

STANCE:

Corner's outside foot is up, with his weight on this foot. Bend at the waist, allow arms to hang down in a relaxed manner. Safety's feet are parallel, weight on the balls of the feet, knees bent slightly. Safety stands more erect. Kat's outside foot is up, with very low stance.

ALIGNMENT:

Corner
1. Vs. a #1 receiver in a tight position, align 2 yards outside #1 receiver and 4-5 yards deep
2. Vs. a #1 receiver who is split 7 or less yards, align 1 yard outside #1, and align 6-7 yards deep
3. Vs. a #1 receiver who is split 7 or more yards, align 1 yard inside #1, and align 6-7 yards deep
4. Vs. a #1 receiver who is positioned within 7 yards of the sideline, never align closer than 7 yards to the sideline

Kat
1. Vs. a #1 receiver in a tight position, align 1 yard outside of #2 receiver and 5 yards deep
2. Vs. a #1 receiver who is split 5 or more yards, align 3 yards outside the #2 receiver and 3-5 yards deep
3. Vs. twins formation, align 1-3 yards inside #2 receiver and 5 yards deep

Free
1. On a cloud call, align in the weak side, Center—guard gap and 7-10 yards deep

2. On a sky call, creep to an alignment on the weak side, tackle and 7-10 yards deep

KEYS:
Strong Corner—Through the tight end to the ball (QB)

Kat—Through the tight end to ball (QB)

Safety—Ball (QB), and #2 receiver on strong side and #1 receiver on weak side

Weak Corner—Ball (QB), and #1 receiver

ASSIGNMENTS:
a. Strong side Corner
1. Run toward (cloud)—force
2. Run toward (sky)—secondary force
3. Run away—safety, last man
4. Pass toward or pocket (cloud)—flat
5. Pass toward or pocket (sky) outside 1/3
6. Pass away—outside 1/3

b. Weak side Corner
1. Run toward (cloud)—force
2. Run toward (sky)—secondary force
3. Run away—safety, last man
4. Pass toward (cloud)—flat
5. Pass toward (sky)—outside 1/3
6. Pass away or pocket—outside 1/3

c. Kat
1. Run toward (cloud)—secondary force
2. Run toward (sky)—force
3. Run away—inside-out force
4. Pass toward or pocket (cloud)—outside 1/3
5. Pass toward or pocket (sky)—flat
6. Pass away—middle 1/3

d. Free
1. Run toward (cloud)—secondary force
2. Run toward (sky)—force
3. Run away—inside-out force
4. Pass toward (sky)—outside 1/3
5. Pass toward (cloud)—outside 1/3
6. Pass away or pocket—middle 1/3

LINEBACKER PLAY:

a. *Sam*
Alignment—40 or 50 alignment
Key—40 or 50 key

Assignment—
1. Drop-back pass—hook to curl
2. Sprint strong—curl, if QB breaks containment you must force
3. Spring weak—back side hook to middle
4. Collision tight end whenever possible.

b. *Mike*   Alignment—40 or 50 alignment
Key—40 or 50 key
Assignment—
1. Drop-back pass—middle
2. Sprint strong—strong side hook
3. Sprint weak—weak side hook

c. *Willie*   Alignment—40 or 50 alignment
Key—40 or 50 key
Assignment—
1. Drop-back pass—curl to flat
2. Sprint strong—back side hook to middle
3. Sprint weak—curl, if QB breaks containment, you must force

Cover II (Figure 7-28)

Cover II is a zone coverage by 5 underneath men, with 2 defensive backs playing 1/2 zones deep. Will be used with any of our fronts. We will always have cloud run support.

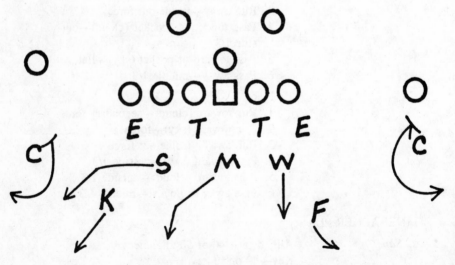

Figure 7-28

SQUAT CORNERS

Stance:	Inside foot back, belly button to the ball. Slight bend in knees, looking straight into the ball
Alignment:	1 yard outside, 5 yards deep
Key:	Through the tight end to the ball. No tight end to your side read QB and ball.

Assignments:

1. Run toward—drive inside of receiver; try to get to L.O.S.; you must close down the running lane. If receiver blocks, shed receiver by getting hands on his shoulder pads. Pull down and to the inside. Do not get blocked inside. Do not get drive too far outside.
2. Run away—check reverse and revolve deep, looking for cut-back. You are safety, last man.
3. Drop-back pass or sprint-out pass toward—you have flat coverage. Step up and molest receiver and funnel him to the inside. You must force receiver out of his normal release whether his release is in or out. Do not allow receiver to get a clean release, jam him. If there is no threat from a second receiver, sink while reading QB's arm motion and drive to the ball. If a second receiver shows (i.e. back flaring), find a happy medium, forcing QB to throw short. Be alert to screens.
4. Sprint-out pass away—deepen with wide receiver, take away throwback. Post and curl. Play deep outside 1/3.
5. If no threat in your zone, keep getting depth.

SAFETYS

Stance:	Slight crouch, inside foot slightly back
Alignment:	12-14 yards deep. Align within relative distance to the other safety, approximately 1-4 yards apart. If ball is in the middle of the field, you should be on the inside part of the hash mark.

Assignments:

1. Run toward—take away halfback pass threat. Drive toward L.O.S. and fill where

needed, usually inside the corner. We always have cloud force.

2. Run away—revolve through middle of the field. You must take away the cut-back with inside-out force.

3. Drop-back pass—get depth and play your 1/2. Must see QB and receiver's releases. If wide receiver releases outside, you must widen; inside release, you should stay inside. Get a jump on the ball by reading QB's head, shoulders, and cocking motion. When QB cocks his arm to throw, you must be moving in that direction prior to release of the ball.

4. Sprint-out pass toward—get depth and widen with the QB. Continue to read the QB and the receivers in your zone. Do not go within 10 yards of the side line unless you read the QB's throwing action.

5. Sprint-out pass away—get depth and revolve into the middle. Be alert for throwback pass.

6. Whenever there is indecision as to whether it is a pass or run—play pass. On all passes be sure to gain depth for crossing routes from opposite side.

7. 2 deep zones will have slight rotation away from weak side—this will give combo look.

LINEBACKER PLAY
SAM

Alignment:	40 or 50 alignment
Key:	40 or 50 key
Assignments:	1. Drop-back pass—attack the tight end. You must be very aggressive in holding up the tight end and do not let him get deep quickly. Get depth and read QB and receiver's routes. Cover receivers, not grass. On drop-back pass, do not cross over hash mark into sideline. If ball is in the middle of the field, get to the inside part of the hash mark.
	2. Sprint-out pass toward—molest tight end's release. Widen with QB. Read QB's

throwing action. If QB breaks containment, you must force.
3. Sprint-out pass away—molest tight end's release. Do not let him run drag pattern. Slide toward the middle, getting depth. Look for throwback. Post or curl.

MIKE

Alignment: 40 or 50 alignment

Key: 40 or 50 key

Assignments:
1. Drop-back pass—drop your leg toward the tight end side of the formation. Get depth by turning your shoulders and running and looking over your shoulder at the QB—back relationship for draw. Search out receivers in your area. Cover receivers, not grass. You should usually be in the middle of the field.
2. Sprint-out pass—drop your leg toward the direction of the sprint-out. Get width with the QB. Be aware of back side drag and throwback patterns.

WILLIE

Alignment: 40 or 50 alignment

Key: 40 or 50 key

Assignments:
1. Drop-back pass—drop your outside leg and turn and sprint, getting depth and width. Keep your eyes on the QB. Do not cross over hash mark into the short side of the field. If ball is in the middle of the field, get to the inside part of the hash mark. Cover receivers, not grass.
2. Sprint-out pass toward—widen with QB. Read QB's throwing action. If QB breaks containment, you must force.
3. Sprint-out pass away—slide toward the middle, getting depth. Look for throwback post or curl.

*Force the offense to dump off to backs. This is the key to this coverage. If we can do this we will be very successful with this coverage.

Cover II Adjustment vs. Twins (Slot) (Figure 7-29)

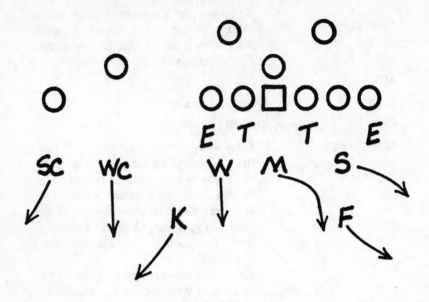

Figure 7-29

Cover III (Figure 7-30)

Cover III is used in long yardage and sure pass situations. This is a zone coverage with the 3 deep zones covered and the Kat and Willie aligned on the 2 wide receivers. Joker would be 5th defensive back brought into game for Willie in passing situations.

Stance:	1. Corners and safety—same as Cover I
	2. Kat and Willie (Joker)—knees bent. Inside foot forward, hands up
Alignment:	1. Corners—same as Cover I except 8-9 yards deep
	2. Kat and Willie (Joker) inside shoulder of wide receiver 5 yards deep
	3. Safety—straight over center 12 yards deep
Key:	1. Corners—ball (QB) and receivers in your zone, through tight end.
	2. Kat and Willie (Joker) tight end to ball (QB)
	3. Free—ball (QB) and all receivers in your zone

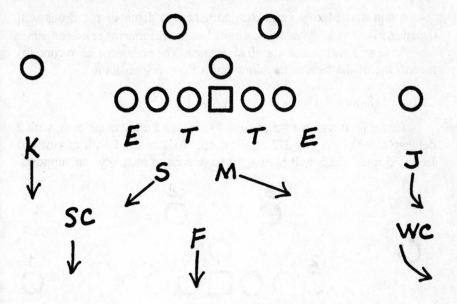

Figure 7-30

Assignment: 1. Corners—run toward—secondary force, run away—safety, last man, pass—vs. all passes play outside 1/3
2. Kat and Willie (Joker)—run toward—force, run away—pursuit, pass—vs. all passes, molest your receiver, force an outside release and play short zone
3. Safety—run—inside-out force, pass—vs. all passes play middle 1/3

LINEBACKER PLAY

1. *Sam*   Alignment—40 alignment
Key—40 key
Assignment—run—defensive call assignment, pass—attack tight end's release, drop to curl, reading QB and receivers

2. *Mike*   Alignment—40 alignment
Key—40 key
Assignment—run—defensive call assignment, pass—read pass and drop to middle, read QB and receivers

*Sam and Mike's vertical alignment and depth of the drops will depend on down and distance, score and time remaining in the half or gam.

*We will always use our 40 alignment. The ends *must* keep containment. One of the tackles has draw and screen responsibility.

Cover IV (Figure 7-31)

Cover IV is a man-to-man coverage by the 5 underneath men, with 2 defensive backs playing 1/2 zones deep. Will be used with any of our fronts. 5 underneath will play aggressive man to man sky run support.

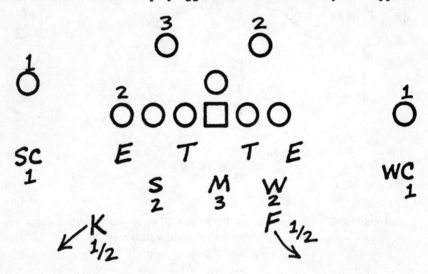

Figure 7-31

SQUAT CORNERS

Stance:	Inside foot back, belly button to the ball. Slight bend in your knees. If we play bump and run, crouch more and align parallel to L.O.S.
Alignment:	1 yard outside, 5 yards deep. If we play bump and run, align with your outside eye on the inside eye of the receiver, 1 yard deep.
Key:	Through the tight end to the ball. No tight end to your side, read QB and ball once you read pass. Your only key is your receiver. If we play bump and run, your only key is your man.

Assignment:	1. Run toward—the safety always has primary run support. React to run as best you can. Fill inside of the safety only if you are sure the ball is going inside. You must play pass until you are sure it is run.
	2. Run away—check reverse and revolve deep, looking for cut-back. You are safety, last man.
	3. Pass—we will always use the hip pocket technique. Bump the receiver and force him to alter his release. Get underneath him and stay between him and the QB. Run stride for stride with him, don't look back for the ball until you hear a "ball" call or the receiver looks back. The receiver usually slows down to catch the ball. Run hard and close down the cushion between you and the receiver.

SAFETIES—KAT—FREE

Stance:	Same as Cover II
Alignment:	Same as Cover II
Key:	Same as Cover II
Assignments:	All assignments are the same except when run is toward you. Give run support aggressively as you have primary force. Force the ball carrier back inside the pursuit.

SAM

Alignment:	40 or 50 alignment
Key:	40 or 50 key, until you read pass. Then tight end becomes your key.
Assignments:	Vs. all passes—you are responsible for tight end man-to-man. Bump him and hinder his release. Get underneath him and stay between him and the QB. You have help deep, so be aggressive. Drive hard with the receiver. Don't look back to L.O.S. until receiver looks back or you hear "run" call by the secondary or other linebackers. If the tight end stays in to block, don't leave him. He will eventually release with a delay pattern.

MIKE

Alignment: 40 or 50 alignment

Key: 40 or 50 key, until you read pass, then #3 receiver, usually the first back out of the backfield to the strong side. Never break up on a back flaring unless you read screen. Move out with the back, staying in front of him, but still get depth so that you can help out on the other receivers. You must always be in a position to tackle a flaring back for no gain. If the back runs a downfield pattern, bump him and get underneath and stay between him and the QB. Don't look back for the ball until the receiver does. Drop to hook zone if your receiver does not enter into pattern.

WILLIE

Alignment: 40 or 50 alignment

Key: 40 or 50 key until you read pass, then #2 receiver becomes your key

Assignments: Vs. all passes—you have the #2 receiver on the weak side, usually the first back out of the backfield to your side. Never break up on a back flaring unless you read screen. Move out with the back, staying in front of him, but still get depth so that you can help out on the other receivers. You must always be in a position to tackle a flaring back for no gain. If the back runs a downfield pattern, bump him and get underneath and stay between him and the QB. Don't look back for the ball until the receiver does. Drop to curl zone if your receiver does not enter into pattern.

Cover IV vs. Twins (Figure 7-32)

On 90 percent of all completed passes the receiver has to slow down to catch the ball. You must discipline yourself not to look back for the ball until the receiver looks back. After the receiver makes his break there will be some separation between you and your man. If you will run hard to close this distance, you will be successful. In stopping the pass attempt the safeties must get a good jump on the ball by reading the QB's throwing action. The safeties must also call out "run" when they run the ball (i.e., draws) and call out "ball" when the ball has been thrown. If the safeties do not do this, we will not be successful with this coverage.

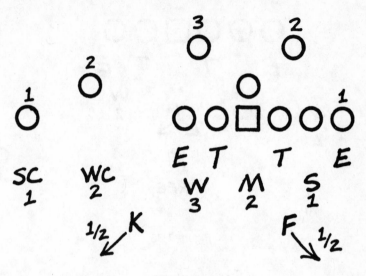

Figure 7-32

Cover V (Figure 7-33)

Cover V is a man-to-man pass coverage based on covering a man, not defending a zone. We will have cloud or sky calls to both sides of the formation.

Stance:	Same as Cover I
Alignment:	*Corners:*

1. Vs. a #1 receiver in a tight position, align 2 yards outside #1 and 4-5 yards deep
2. Vs. a #1 receiver who is split 5 or more yards, align either 1 yard inside or outside depending on the situation, 5-7 yards deep. Follow sideline rule
3. Vs. a #1 receiver who is split 9 or more yards, align 1 yard inside #1, and align 5-7 yards deep

Kat:
1. 1 yard inside or outside #2 receiver on strong side, 4-6 yards deep, depending on situation

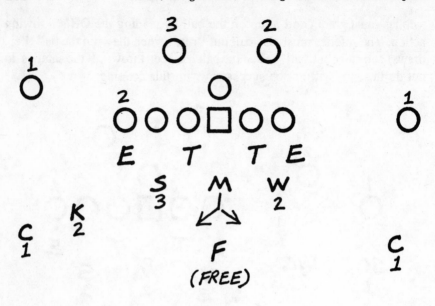

Figure 7-33

Assignment:

Free:
Same as Cover I
1. Same as Cover I until you read pass, then key on your man. Free safety reads QB and all receivers who threaten the middle 1/3

Corners:
1. Run—same as Cover I (sky, cloud)
2. Pass—if #1 receiver releases downfield, cover him man-to-man. If #1 receiver blocks, make sure he does not release late, then you are free and play free in the deep outside 1/3

Kat:
1. Run—same as Cover I (sky, cloud)
2. Pass—if #2 receiver releases downfield, cover him man-to-man. If #2 receiver blocks, make sure he does not release late, then you are free, help out where needed.

Free:
1. Run—same as Cover I (sky, cloud)

2. Pass—drive back to the middle 1/3 keying the QB and receivers threatening the middle 1/3. Don't let any receiver get behind you.

Cover V

COVER V LINEBACKER PLAY

SAM

Alignment:	40 or 50 alignment
Key:	40 or 50 key until you read pass then your key is #3 receiver strong side, usually the first back out of the backfield
Assignment:	1. If #3 releases into the pattern, cover him man-to-man
	2. If #3 blocks, make sure he doesn't release late, then drop into curl area and help out, reading QB and receivers

MIKE

Alignment:	40 or 50 alignment
Key:	40 or 50 key until you read pass, then your key is QB and receivers
Assignment:	1. If both backs release to the same side, you cover the second back man-to-man
	2. Otherwise drop to middle and help out, reading QB and receivers

WILLIE

Alignment:	40 or 50 alignment
Key:	40 or 50 key until you read pass, then your key is #2 receiver weak side, usually the first back out of the backfield
Assignment:	1. If #2 releases into the pattern, cover him man-to-man
	2. If #2 blocks make sure he does not release late, then drop into curl area and help out, reading QB and receivers

Linebackers will switch assignments when 1 or more linebackers are involved in a stunt.

Cover V—No Free

Change up in case of linebacker stunt or to create immediate double coverage on specific receiver. Free would either pick up receiver of stunting linebacker or go to help cover key receiver.

I. DEFENSIVE LINE

The controlling of the line of scrimmage is the most important factor in determining the outcome of any football game. This is what the game of football is all about, the hitting and physical contact that make football such a special game.

In many defenses the main responsibility of the defensive linemen is to keep the offensive linemen from blocking the linebackers. But in our multiple 4-3 defense the front 4 must be active and aggressive, attacking the offense and creating problems for the offensive blocking patterns. We must force the offense into 2nd-and-long, and 3rd-and-long situations through the use of aggressive stunts and blitz. Ours is a coordinated defense with everyone reading his keys and then attacking the football.

If the front 4 are tough and aggressive at all times, all teams that we play will have trouble moving the ball. The opposition's running attack will not get started and an aggressive pass rush throws off the timing of the opponent's passing game.

Your responsibilities, keys, and alignments will change according to the defensive fronts and stunts called and you must know your rules.

If you are going to have a strong team, a great deal depends on the defensive front 4. Take pride in how hard you work and your team and personal goals will be reached.

II. DEFENSIVE END AND TACKLE PLAY (1 or 3 ALIGNMENT)

1. Stance: 3-or-4 point stance, inside foot back, feet spread shoulder-width, back flat, head up and shoulders square to L.O.S.
2. Alignment:
   a. 1 alignment—your outside eye on the inside eye of the offensive lineman
   b. 3 alignment—your inside eye on the outside eye of the offensive lineman
3. Key: head of defensive lineman
4. Defensive charge: attack movement of blocker by stepping with near foot and deliver a forearm shiver with near arm, using far hand to

deliver a blow to the helmet or shoulder pad of blocker, staying square to L.O.S. Maintain leverage under offensive shoulder pads.

5. Reaction to key:

   a. Head fires straight: attack movement by stepping with near forearm and shoulder, deliver a hard blow, being sure to stop blocker from getting to your body. Take second step with far foot to square-up stance. Locate ball and pursue.

   b. Head fires straight with double-team: use technique outlined above, until you see or feel second blocker. Then 2 techniques are available:

      (1) Shoulder dip—drop shoulder toward double-team, splitting double-team. Don't give ground. Do not spin out.

      (2) Grab grass—hit ground, keeping feet moving upfield—don't give ground!

   c. Head fires right or left: blocker's head to your left or right. Explode into blocker. As you read his head, work laterally to the direction of the blocker's head as you locate the ball. Stay low, keeping your shoulders square and legs free. Keep blocker from blocking our linebackers. Attack trap block head-on, creating a pile-up.

   d. Scramble block: scramble block can originate from straight fire out or right-left fire out. Force head and shoulders into ground with hand shiver. You may have to give a little ground to stop blocker from getting into your legs. Protect your body and legs. Stay square to L.O.S. and pursue.

   e. Blocker pull outside: balance up and follow blocker's pull to outside with flat pursuit course. Play through face of blocker blocking down. Locate ball and get in good pursuit angle. Beware of cross block.

   f. Blocker pull inside: balance up and close down hard. Beware of back or lineman trying to cut you off. Locate ball and get in good pursuit angle.

   g. Blocker sets up for pass block: as you come off ball on your initial charge, get your hands on him quickly and get rid of blocker by using different pass rush techniques. As passer cocks his arm to pass, throw your hands in the air as high as possible. (Do not leave your feet until ball is thrown.) Make QB "throw out of a well," tackle QB high, through head and shoulders. If ball is thrown, turn immediately and pursue it. Be aware of contain responsibilities.

III. DEFENSIVE END TECHNIQUE VS. TIGHT END

(Defensive end on weak side uses same techniques, vs. offensive tackle) 4 ALIGNMENT.

1. Stance: same as head up, using 3-point stance.

2. Alignment: your inside shoulder on tight end's outside shoulder, angles slightly in.

3. Key: tight end's head.

4. Defensive charge: react to tight end's movement by taking a step with your inside foot to collision the tight end with a forearm shiver with your inside arm.

5. Reaction to key:
   a. Drive block or turn-out block—step with inside foot to meet blocker with forearm shiver under his shoulder pads. Fight pressure through blocker's head, keeping outside leverage keep off-tackle hold narrow. Fold inside only when you are sure the ball is going inside.
   b. Hook block—you must never be hooked! Attack blocker with forearm shiver and control his head. Do not allow blocker to get on the outside of your body. Keep outside control, locate ball and pursue.
   c. Tight end releases inside to block or inside pass release—collision the tight end and knock him off balance. Read into the backfield to determine if it is pass or run.
   Vs. pass—continue into predetermined pass rush technique, keeping containment.
   Vs. run—determine blocking scheme. Will probably be kickout block by the guard or lead back. Attack the blocker.
   d. Option play—you have the QB vs. the option. We will play the slam technique. Attack the QB immediately and violently. Force the QB to pitch the ball prematurely and inaccurately. We want you to intimidate the QB and cause a fumble by tackling high.
   e. Action goes away—you have reverse responsibility. Trail the play, no deeper than the ball, until the ball crosses the L.O.S. Then get in the proper pursuit angle.

IV. READ TECHNIQUE OF DEFENSIVE TACKLE

Responsibility—tackles will never be expected to control both sides of an offensive lineman. The side you are to control will be indicated as such:
   a. *Tom*—both tackles will control the *outside* of the linemen they align on.
   b. *Tim*—both tackles will control the *inside* of the linemen they align on.
   c. *Toss*—both tackles will control the *strong side* of the linemen they align on.
   d. *Twin*—both tackles will control the *weak side* of the linemen they align on.
1. Stance: same as 1 or 3 alignment
2. Alignment: 2 alignment—nose to nose with offensive lineman.
3. Key: offensive lineman's head

4. Defensive charge: attack movement of blocker, step with foot toward the side the blocker's head goes to. Attack with either a hand or forearm shiver, followed quickly with your opposite foot to get a parallel base. You must control the side of the blocker you are assigned to.

5. Reaction to key: same as 1 or 3 technique

V. PASS RUSH

1. Hints:
   a. Crowd the ball
   b. Get into sprinter's stance
   c. Key the ball (when it moves, you move)
   d. Get close to the blocker
   e. Always have a planned rush vs. the blocker
   f. "Fight" your way in, never give up
   g. Tackle high. Ends must keep QB in the pocket
2. Pass rush techniques:
   a. Butt
      (1) On snap, accelerate into blocker with forehead (clash headgear) and double-hand shiver to drive him backward. Either push blocker into passer or slip around blocker.
   b. Kung Fu
      (1) Get close to blocker
      (2) Grab shoulder pad either side with one hand, pull toward you, turning his shoulders
      (3) Swing opposite arm across blocker's body (swim), follow with your body to get by blocker
   c. Hook and spin
      (1) Attack one side of blocker, getting him to turn his shoulders.
      (2) Get close to blocker.
      (3) As blocker opens to that side, thrust elbow to rear and spin your body to opposite side, using elbow and arm to pull yourself by blocker
   d. Race horse
      (1) Race straight through outside shoulder of blocker after giving inside head fake
      (2) If contact is made, slide by his outside by turning your shoulders. Don't break stride

I. LINEBACKERS

Ideally, this position should be filled by a man who possesses the abilities of both a defensive back and a defensive lineman. Strength, quickness, durability, awareness, and a desire for contact—these are the qualities needed by the linebacker. Strength is a must in the ability to ward off the block, make the hit, and prevent that extra yard after contact. Quickness is as vital to rushing defense as it is to passing defense. We expect linebackers to make the greatest number of hits and thus durability is essential. Blocking angles vary so greatly that linebackers must be able to withstand a great deal of physical abuse.

The most important knowledge for sound defensive football is a constant awareness of what the opponent must gain in order to maintain possession. The linebackers must realize down and distance, field position and opposition tendency. The ability to react and the instinct for finding the ball are two other important factors in playing good defensive football. The linebackers are the heart and soul of a strong defense. They set the tempo for the rest of the squad, both in practices and in games. Aggressiveness is essential to play linebacker for us. The linebacker must strike a balance between playing under control with knowledge of his assignments and playing with reckless abandon.

Linebackers will have a variety of alignments, keys and responsibilities in our multiple 4-3 defense. They must learn their assignments perfectly to play with the confidence necessary to dominate their positions. Everyone has the will to win, but the linebacker must have the will to prepare to win.

II. GENERAL LINEBACKER RULES

1. Stance: Eagle position
2. Key:
   a. Over uncovered lineman—lineman's head, near back and ball
   b. Over covered lineman—near back and ball
In reading keys, you must develop the ability to read as much as possible from them to get an understanding of the offensive play.
3. General Responsibilities:
   a. Control primary area of responsibility.
   b. Play cutback lane on offside plays.
   c. Pursue aggressively on outside plays, but don't overrun.
   d. Hook, curl and flat responsibilities in zone pass coverages, depending on coverage, usually 12 yards deep.
   e. #2 or #3 when dictated by man coverage.
   f. #1 vs. all options (exception—from 50 and 50 over Sam has #2).

III. SAM AND WILLIE—VS. TIGHT END OR SLOT

1. Stance: 2 points, feet even, shoulder width, knees bent, weight on balls of feet. Shoulders square to L.O.S., hands cocked in front of chest, eyes on 3rd man (T.E. or slot).

2. Alignment: Inside eye on outside eye of 3rd man. May be wider according to quickness.

3. Key: head of 3rd man.

4. Defensive charge: react to movement of third man by taking a step with the same foot as direction of tight end or slot's head. Use hand shiver or forearm shiver to attack, always keep shoulders square to L.O.S., locate ball.

5. Reaction to key:

   a. Drive block or turn-out block—step with inside foot to meet blocker with forearm shiver under his shoulder pads. Bring outside foot up to balance base and separate blocker by using hands. Fight pressure through blocker's head, keep outside leverage. If ball crosses neutral point on L.O.S. inside of you, fold inside and help make play.

   b. Hook block—step with outside foot to get width. Attack blocker with hand shiver to control his head. Do not allow blocker to get outside of your body. Keep outside control, locate ball and pursue.

   c. Third man blocks inside—take shuffle step inside using hand shiver to knock blocker off his path. Stay balanced and keep shoulders square to L.O.S. Look for block by guard or back. Maintain outside control.

   d. Arc release—step with outside foot to get width and use hand shiver on third man's outside release. Ride laterally for 2 yards, always looking back inside. Then squat and play your basic responsibility.

   e. Option play—our option responsibilities—dive man is #1, QB is #2, and pitch man is #3. You will normally have #2. Change up would make Willie on #3 and free will take #2

      (1) Slam-attack the QB immediately and violently. Force him to pitch prematurely and inaccurately. We want you to intimidate the QB and cause a fumble. Tackle high.

   f. Pass drop—hold up third man on L.O.S. as long as possible with hand shiver. Keep eye on QB, take open step, getting width and depth, checking receivers in your area. When QB sets up, you set up and break on his arm motion, usually 12 yards depth. Be aware of draw and screen.

   g. Sprint-out pass toward you—if the QB breaks containment of defensive end, take path to maintain outside relationship on the ball. Penetrate to the ball and make passer pull up.

IV. SAM AND WILLIE VS. OFFENSIVE TACKLE

1. Stance: Eagle position
2. Alignment:
   Sam—3, alignment, 2 to 4 yards off the L.O.S.
   Willie in 40 and 50 front—B gap, 2 to 4 yards off the L.O.S.
   Willie in 40 over and 50 over front—3 alignment on the guard, 2 to 4 yards off the L.O.S.
3. Key:
   Sam—tackle's head, to ball
   Willie (a) 40 or 50—tackle's head to ball
         (b) 40 over or 50 over—guard's head to ball
4. Reaction to key:
   a. Drive block—attack the fire-out movement of the tackle by stepping up aggressively. Take on the tackle with your inside forearm and shoulder. Drive this forearm shiver under his pads while driving your opposite hand through his shoulder pads or helmet. Bring your other foot up to balance. Keep shoulders square. Fight pressure through the blocker's head, keeping outside leverage. Squeeze the area between you and the inside defense.
   b. Cut-off block—take lateral step in direction of blocker's movement. Take on block with opposite forearm, bringing your other hand to attack blocker's pads or helmet. Stay square to L.O.S. Locate ball and pursue.
   c. Drive block with double team—attack the seam between the blockers, split them by dropping your outside shoulder. Do not spin out.
   d. Down block by tight end—attack the blocker by fighting across his head. Stay low and keep your shoulders square to L.O.S.
   e. Pass block—when the blocker's head pops up you read pass. Plant and pivot your inside foot and immediately check the tight end's release. Our defensive end will have funneled the tight end to you. Attack the tight end's release. Read the angle of drop by the QB to help determine your angle of pass drop (pocket, sprint-out to or away).

V. MIKE VS. CENTER FOR 40 AND 50 FRONT

1. Stance: Eagle position
2. Alignment: 2-4 yards off L.O.S., head-up on the center
3. Key: ball and near back through the center's head
4. Reaction to key:
   a. Drive block-attack the fire-out movement of the center by stepping up aggressively, reading the flow of the backs. Take on the center with the foot and forearm opposite the flow of the backs. Drive this forearm

shiver under his pads, while driving your other hand through his shoulder pads or helmet. Bring your other foot up to balance. Keep shoulders square, destroy the blocker, locate the ball and pursue.

b. Scoop block—take lateral step in direction of center's movement. Take on block with opposite forearm, bringing your other hand to attack center's pads or helmet. Stay square to L.O.S. Locate ball and pursue.

c. Down block by guard—attack down block by driving your play side forearm through the guard's head, working across his face. Stay square, locate ball, pursue and tackle.

VI. HIP ALIGNMENT FOR WILLIE VS. SPLIT END

1. Stance: Eagle position
2. Alignment: 1 yard deeper than heels of defensive end, 1-2 yards outside
3. Key: ball and near back
4. Reaction to key:
   a. Read your key, maintain outside pressure and leverage in order to keep the area between you and your inside pursuit as small as possible.
   b. Off-tackle-lead blocker (back or guard) approaches you on a definite inside-out path (no threat to outside). Meet blocker with a powerful inside shoulder-forearm charge, keep outside foot back, shoulders square to L.O.S. Do not turn in. Keep in position to release outside if runner bounces to outside.
   c. Sweep-lead blocker approaches you on definite outside path. Penetrate into the offensive backfield and maintain an outside position on the lead blocker. Force the blocker to commit his block as soon as possible. Keep the area between you and your pursuit as small as possible or else force the ball carrier deep and wide.

*Additional alignments
Walk-away—split the distance between defensive end and wide receiver, 2-3 yards deep.
Hold-up—1 alignment on wide receiver, forcing outside release.

VII. PASS TECHNIQUES FOR ALL LINEBACKERS

1. As soon as a linebacker recognizes a pass play, he should call it out and start running to his area of responsibility as fast as possible. Don't drift, sprint.
2. Turn and run laterally looking over your inside shoulder at relationship of QB to backs for possible draw.

3. As you are going to your zone, look for receivers coming into your area, at the same time watching the QB (head on a swivel).

4. Keep dropping as long as QB is not set, when QB sets, you set (up to 12 yards).

5. You must react to all looks of the QB to your area. When QB looks, sprint at an angle to make the interception in front of the receiver, at its highest point.

6. Communicate. Let adjacent defenders know if a receiver is crossing into his area.

7. If a receiver crosses a linebacker's path, he should be knocked to the ground or at least off stride.

8. Once the ball is thrown, all linebackers must be running at full speed to the ball until it falls to the ground.

9. Read the angle of release by the QB to determine if it is a dropback or sprint-out pass. Adjust your area to this action.

10. If QB drops deeper than normal, look for screen.

11. Keep your feet moving at all times.

12. On man coverage, look right at the receiver's numbers, concentrate on him.

13. Strip the receiver by taking away his upfield arm. Punish any receiver who catches the ball.

14. Don't cover grass, search out receivers in your area. Collision receivers.

15. Concentrate, break to the ball, make the big play.

16. Go for the receiver when he is underneath you. Go for the ball when he is even or has beaten you.

VIII. COVER I PASS RESPONSIBILITIES

Sam Pass Responsibilities—Cover I

1. Read the release of the third man. Hinder his release as much as possible. Plant and pivot off your inside foot and sprint to your curl zone, depth of 10-12 yards. If tight end releases outside, be aware of flanker on an inside route.

2. On sprint-out strong, widen with QB. If he breaks contain, come up and force from an outside in position.

3. On sprint-out weak, drop back inside, watching for T.E. drag and throwback post to flanker.

4. Don't break up on a back flaring until QB turns shoulder toward the back.

Mike Pass Responsibilities—Cover I

1. Read pass, open step to tight end side. Be aware of T.E. Drag and draw.

2. Get depth of 12 yards quickly. React to routes of receivers in your area.

3. On sprint-out, widen with QB to hook zone, look for receivers curling or backside drag.

4. Never let T.E. cross your face.

Willie Pass Responsibilities—Cover I

1. Read pass, open step to outside and move to curl area 10-12 yards deep. Be aware of split end curl and near back out of backfield.

2. Don't break up on back flaring until QB turns shoulders toward the back.

3. On sprint-out weak, widen with QB. If he breaks contain, come up and force from an outside in position.

4. On sprint-out strong, drop back inside, watch for throwback post to split end.

5. If not threatened by an outside route by the split end or near back, squeeze back to the inside.

I. DEFENSE SECONDARY

You have the toughest assignment on a football team. One mistake by you and our opponent has a long gain or touchdown. Most football games are won or lost on pass defense. On practically every scoring drive, a key gain will be made on a completed pass. The game will be more open than ever in the future, with the pass playing a leading role in our opponent's offenses. In order for you to play in our defensive secondary, you must have a complete understanding of the following phases of secondary play:

    a. Understand our pass defensive calls.

    b. Know exactly where and how to align.

    c. Recognize the pass or run and the pass patterns.

    d. Know the responsibilities and coverages versus the pass or run and follow your rules of reacting to keys, angle of pursuit and rotation.

To successfully fulfill the above mentioned phases of defensive secondary play, you must possess the physical aspects of agility, quickness and aggressiveness, the mental aspects of concentration and complete knowledge of your assignment as well as what the other defenders are doing, and the emotional aspects of enthusiasm, desire, and spirit necessary to be a winner.

Work as a unit, take pride in what the defensive secondary can do. You must have a burning desire to play pass defense and to excel.

II. GENERAL RULES FOR DEFENSIVE BACKS

A. Always know down, distance, time and position (vertical and lateral) on the field.

B. Be aware of speed of receiver.

C. Always go for the ball and intercept it high. Be aggressive. But go through the receiver.

D. If passer fumbles the ball and receivers are downfield, cover receivers until whistle blows.

E. Deep backs should never go for man hooking in front of you until the ball is in the air. Keep your cushion.

F. Good position on the pass receiver is important.

G. Concentration is vital to all phases of great pass defense.

H. You must constantly talk on defense.

I. Punish the receiver who has caught the football.

J. If your receiver is going to catch the ball and you have no chance to intercept or deflect the pass, make certain that you tear away the upfield arm. This is the arm that is the farthest from the flight of the ball.

K. It is essential in man-to-man coverage for you to always see the man you are covering as you look for the ball. Never look away from the receiver for the ball.

L. Repeat to yourself the type of coverage and your keys.

M. Reading your keys demands strict mental discipline.

N. If you get beat, run with the receiver and look for the ball as he looks for the ball. 90 percent of the time he will have to slow up to catch the ball.

O. Balance up to a hit position as you approach the ball carrier. Tackle him high, drive through the ball carrier. You must arm wrap and wait for help.

P. Be mentally and physically tough!

III. CORNER (JACK)

A. Run defense "onside" with a cloud call.
  1. Take shuffle-step, read run on the end of the shuffle. Read your keys.
  2. Keep outside foot back, outside arm free.

3. Come up at a slight angle to L.O.S. to close down area from you to defensive end or linebacker.
4. Vs. crackblock—close down with the crack man, yell crack to alert linebackers, Kat or safety. May use cloud call.
5. Never penetrate more than 3 yards across the L.O.S.
6. Keep shoulders square to L.O.S.
7. Balance up to a hit position.
8. Don't take eye off blocker too soon, control blocker, then turn attention to ball carrier.
9. When one-on-one with outside ball carrier, use the sideline if within 5 yards of it.

B. Run defense "onside" with a sky call.
1. Take shuffle-step.
2. Read the QB and eligible receivers.
3. When you read run, you will support inside or outside off the Kat or safety.
4. Only support inside if the ball definitely is forced inside.
5. Get depth so you can oversee the situation.

C. Run defense "offside."
1. Take shuffle-step.
2. Read your key.
3. Take 3 steps back before you start on pursuit course.
4. Keep checking receivers on your side as you go on pursuit path, glance ahead of ball for possible reverses or deep receivers coming from opposite side through your area.
5. Rotate through middle 1/3, then evaluate where play will end up. Watch cutback, don't let ball cross your face.
6. Play pass until ball crosses L.O.S.
7. As ball carrier breaks downfield, get head-up on the ball and force it into the near sideline.
8. If not completely sure it is a run, stay in your deep 1/3 and get a late start on pursuit path. When in doubt, get depth.

D. Pass defense—Deep 1/3 assignment.
1. At end of shuffle, continue deep into your outside 1/3. Key the #1 and #2 receivers. Proper position in your 1/3 depends on direction of ball, field position, yard line, hash mark, and formation.
2. Stay deeper than the deepest receiver in your area or one coming into your area. No one gets behind you.
3. As you go back, keep balanced and square so you can react quickly to either side.
4. Split 2 receivers breaking deep in your zone.
5. With no receivers breaking deep into your zone, you can pull up quicker to help on the short or inside patterns.
6. Always keep QB in sight by knowing where he is looking to throw the ball.

E. Pass Defense—Flat Assignment—Cloud.
   1. If any of the receivers to your side release, play pass first, at end of your shuffle-step level off for flat, concentrating on QB and #1 to #2 receivers.
   2. If the outside receiver goes deep, hinder him, and check the #2 receiver. If both go deep, you get deeper in the flat unless #3 comes into your flat.
   3. If 2 receivers enter your zone, be in a position to cover the widest receiver.
   4. Vs. a swing pass or screen, maintain outside leverage, forcing the receiver to the inside pursuit.
   5. When QB gets ready to throw, be ready to get a jump on the ball in any direction.

IV. FREE AND KAT

A. Run defense—"onside" (sky).
   1. Take shuffle-step, read on end of shuffle.
   2. Key free—QB (ball). Kat—through tight end to near back.
   3. Never penetrate more than 3 yards across the L.O.S.
   4. Keep outside foot back, outside arm free.
   5. Keep shoulders square to L.O.S.
   6. Vs. crackback block—fight through the crackback by going through him with your outside shoulder, striking a blow.
   7. Balance up to a hit position.
   8. Don't take eye off the blocker too soon, control blocker, then turn attention to ball carrier.
   9. When one-on-one with outside running ball carrier, use the sideline if within 5 yards of it.
B. Run defense "onside" (cloud) secondary force.
   1. Take shuffle-step, read on end of shuffle.
   2. Key—Kat—through tight end to near back—free—QB (ball).
   3. Only support inside if the ball definitely is forced inside by the corner.
   4. Get depth so you can oversee the situation.
C. Run defense—"offside."
   1. Take shuffle-step, read run at end of shuffle.
   2. Key the QB and receivers.
   3. Always start for your deep 1/3 zone first.
   4. Always stay behind the ball, never let it cross your face.
   5. Maintain an inside-outside position.
D. Pass defense—flat assignment (sky call) (Pocket or sprint to Kat).
   1. Take shuffle-step, read pass on end of shuffle, check QB and receivers.

2. If 2 receivers enter your zone, be in a position to cover the widest receiver.
3. Vs. a swing pass or screen, maintain outside leverage, forcing the receiver to the inside pursuit.
4. If no one shows in the flat area, get depth and keep square to L.O.S., look inside for crossing receiver.
5. When QB gets ready to throw, be ready to get a jump on the ball in any direction.

E. Pass—toward Kat or Free (cloud).
1. Take shuffle-step, read pass on end of shuffle-step, check QB and receivers.
2. Concentrate first on outside receiver.
3. You are mainly concerned with who is breaking deep in your zone.
4. If there are 2 receivers breaking deep in your area, split them.
5. If there are no receivers breaking deep in your area, you can pull up quicker to help on the short and inside patterns.
6. Always keep QB in view. Know where he is looking to throw the ball.
7. Stay deeper than the deepest receiver in your area or coming into your area. No one gets behind you.

F. Pass—middle 1/3 assignment (sprint away from Kat, pocket or sprint strong for free).
1. Take shuffle-step, read pass on end of shuffle, check QB and receivers.
2. Key first on #2 receiver to determine your angle to the middle 1/3.
3. Always be aware of back side post pattern.
4. If there are 2 receivers breaking deep into your area, try to split them.
5. As you go back, keep balanced and square so you can react quickly to either side. Let no one get behind you.
6. Always keep the QB in your line of vision, get a jump on the ball.

Chapter 8

PRACTICE AND SCOUTING SUMMARY— TOTAL PRACTICE PREPARATION FOR THE YEAR-AROUND PROGRAM

WHEN THE FOOTBALL COACHING STAFF ASSEMBLES during the last days of August or the first of September, it is necessary to wrap up overall season planning. The staff at this time must have studied all charts, movies, and statistics from the previous season.

First, it follows that if two teams are equal in ability going into a game, the difference might lie in which team gets the most out of its practice sessions during the week. This does not necessarily mean having the squad engage in a lot of hitting, scrimmaging, or full team work throughout the week. Organization and effective use of time are the keys to championship games. All coaches do the big things. The winners also make sure the little things get done right.

Second, practice variations are vital. Different approaches to practice should be studied so that routine boredom does not set in. When the team hits the field, the start of practice should be varied. This can be accomplished by having group calisthenics, team calisthenics, and a running program which can be done by positions or by teams. If a coach is stressing heavy conditioning, practice should begin with interval running sessions to tire the team initially prior to practice. Whatever is done, practice should be varied even for the mere sake of variation. Conditioning should be done at the end of practice for the most part. Individual drills and technique work should be completed when the athlete is at his freshest. We are not talking about drastic changes. A team must know what to expect each day and develop a rhythm.

Third, set a tempo and attempt to maintain it throughout the practice session. Water breaks now are highly recommended in the middle of the practice period; however, a coach must be cautious that he does not lose tempo following the break. Five minutes should be allowed for the break, and the team then should be required to pick up the practice schedule and tempo immediately.

Fourth, we believe that high school players must play the actual game a lot more than is necessary at the college level. More complete scrimmages must be scheduled for the beginning player so he can experience the total "feel" more than he does during breakdown drill work. Confidence for the individual, which can be instilled during a practice session, is vital for top game performance.

Fifth, it is the responsibility of the coach to keep everyone involved and on the move during each practice session. Coaches often want to teach only their top players at the expense of training the lesser squad members. However, we owe it to ourselves and to the participants to coach everyone who is in a uniform. Injuries occur often in this game and you had better have every player on your team ready. Under pressure, these people will usually come through quite well.

Sixth, and most important, is the time schedule. Punctuality is the key and cannot be violated. A team must be both on and off the field at a predetermined time to maintain good morale. If practice is set between the hours of 4 p.m. and 6 p.m., this does not mean it is from 4 p.m. to 6:15 p.m. If a coach is consistent regarding the time the team is dismissed, then he can always demand that the players report for practice on time and work hard. This precise scheduling also aids the efficiency of the assistant coaches in the time allotments for their individual drills. Assign the time allotment to the manager, and instruct him to give a five-minute warning prior to each time allotment break. Nothing can kill morale more rapidly than by breaking down the time schedule on the field. Don't drag practice along trying to perfect something that you planned ten minutes for and have not completed. You have at least six groups working and the rest can't wait for one problem that probably won't be corrected that day, anyway.

Seventh, a coach must set certain specific discipline standards that he wants to maintain at all times during practices or game situations. These will vary; however, here are some examples: don't allow players to sit down on the practice field; chin straps must be buttoned throughout the entire practice except perhaps during the water break; shirt-tails in at all times; run full-speed from one drill to another; jog to and from the practice field; players must properly address all of their coaches either by the titles "Mr." or "Coach," and maintain a clean locker room, one in which the team can take pride. There are numerous other standards which might be included. Perhaps some coaches want to enforce only a few. But whatever they are, the enforcement must be consistent in maintaining a top standard of morale and performance. Whatever standards are required, punctuality is the *one* that must be included. If a player is late to practice, he should be punished so he will be on time at the next practice; in all fairness to the rest of the squad, one or more players cannot be allowed to be late. We have found that the fewer rules we have, the fewer problems we have. We also have a rule that helps us in discipline problems: "We want to hear the reason why, but there will never be an excuse of any type accepted!"

Eighth, and this is a must—practice whatever will be used in the game. This may appear to be very obvious; however, it must be emphasized. Often, we coaches tend to set a complete running and pass game and will practice each one of the component parts equally in time. This is very impractical if there are certain plays that will not be used in the upcoming game. We believe strongly that coaches should call the plays during a game. They should be aware of the plays that should be practiced. If the coach is calling a good number of pass plays, then those are the plays that should be practiced.

ORGANIZE—DEMONSTRATE—EXECUTE

Drills can be more efficiently conducted if players and coaches know the designated places for their execution. We divide the practice field into seven drill stations—for offensive backs, offensive linemen, receivers, QB's, and three defensive areas.

A good habit to develop when introducing a drill is to demonstrate it first. It is much easier for players to grasp a drill if they have seen it executed. Demonstration must stress objectives and technique and should include: (1) Oral explanation of drill; (2) Walking through steps; and (3) Full-scale active demonstration. As these are concluded, emphasis on technique can be highlighted.

Instruction, preceded by an explanation regarding second-effort aspects of the exercise, should follow initial teaching of the drill.

It is suggested that coaches who cannot effectively demonstrate a drill not try to do so. Instead, call upon a capable player. It is also recommended that bags, dummies, sleds, and other teaching apparatus, rather than players, be used when demonstrating, if possible.

PRACTICE-PERFECT

We recommend keeping players in lines whenever possible. In addition, we discipline those who talk to others during a drill. Our staff insists upon hustle and all-out performance every minute. Above all, we never permit a player to execute a drill incorrectly.

There are many approaches to developing spirit in drills. In any case, a coach must first convince players that drills will help improve their play. After athletes accept this, they must see results. They want to see their progress on a chart, know they are executing a skill faster or blocking better. Besides the youngster himself knowing of improvement, it is wise to keep other players posted. When this pride in accomplishment is motivated in a few players, the entire squad will be affected and uplifted.

DRILLS THAT MAKE THE DIFFERENCE

No. 1: Drills function better if they are kept short and progressive. Most drills can fulfill their purposes in a five-minute period. Activities lasting longer should be repeated less frequently to discourage boredom.

No. 2: Equipment for drills should be available at coaching station prior to players' arrival. Items such as dummies, air bags, sled, tires, ropes, footballs, should be convenient for immediate use.

No. 3: All players run to and from drill area. Stragglers must be disciplined. Coach responsible for drill should lead group to station if possible.

No. 4: Before introducing drill, demonstrate procedure or technique.

No. 5: Be sure goals are being met and drill is realistic.

No. 6: Use starting count to begin drills and whistle to end them.

No. 7: Never allow too many athletes to be working in drill at one time.

No. 8: Coach should position himself in most advantageous position possible to witness activity.

SCOUTING

If you don't have a well-organized scouting program, you won't be a winner. There are four major areas of concern:

1. Offense
2. Defense
3. Kicking Game
4. Personnel

Untold hours and money are spent in an attempt to arrive at a solution that will provide the tools for a winning effort.

The choosing of an efficient scout, the use of films, methods of organizing and evaluating both the off-season and in-season scouting evaluation systems, total staff environment, selective scouting forms and their use; what to ask the scout when he returns to campus, sample scouting reports, preparing the scout for his assignment, and some of the new scouting trends, including computerized scouting, and cross-year evaluations, are all important.

Scouting obviously differs, depending upon the coaching level. However, knowing what the opponent is going to do is something every coach wants to know. The methods and procedures that are used obviously will depend upon the available money as well as the abilities of the scouting personnel.

Many young coaches point to their lack of funds or lack of available scouting personnel as a reason for decreased scouting emphasis. We believe these excuses are unnecessary, and that a coach at any level can organize a workable system.

Scouting, as is true in so many other areas of football, has undergone a great change in the past few years. We have come to the conclusion that a competent scout can sit in a football stadium, or he can perform his responsibilities in a film screening room. We believe that the combination of the two techniques supplies the best possible information. If we had to make a choice, we believe that a better evaluation can be obtained through the use of films. Every aspect of the opponent's offensive and defensive system can be studied and analyzed in detail by using films. Plays and defenses can be run back and forth many times to determine whether there is some key to aid us in our preparation. Make sure there is a league rule that makes film exchange mandatory. We have seen coaches who try to hide what they are doing. In our opinion this type of behavior is neither professional nor very good coaching policy. The people who coach good, solid football have no real secrets. Football, in general, is benefited by a game between two well-prepared teams. Films usually are more than adequate to provide thorough examinations of the opponents.

When exchanging films it is important to have a well-organized system of procurement as well as an efficient means of keeping track of your own films.

Even though we prefer the use of films, we also are aware of the importance of having a staff member scout each opponent. Our current scouting program consists of a two-man approach which allows our personnel to observe each opponent the week prior to the scheduled game. This technique provides a necessary continuity and basis for comparison. One scout concentrates on the opponent's offense, the other on the defense. Another advantage of using the two-scout system is their aid in the subsequent week of practice when they supervise the scout teams to prepare your offensive and defensive players. These scouts also are responsible for written and oral reports to be presented to the other staff members. The head coach and coordinators should present the report to the team. In all scouting procedures, it must be remembered that it is not only the amount of knowledge to be gained by the coaches that is important; it is how much of this knowledge can be translated and communicated to the players.

Scouting at N.M.S.U. begins sometime during the month of May when preliminary scouting assignments are issued for the following fall. We take out last fall's films and scouting reports and start preparing for next fall.

The preliminary scouting directive is issued to the staff late in the spring, and assignments are made regarding who will be responsible for reviewing the films and who will perform the on-the-scene scouting.

We are aware that most high school coaches are very conscious of the importance of scouting and like to do as much of the actual man-looks themselves as possible. The hard-working coach will see films of as many as three or four games a weekend to try to keep up with his opponents' progress. This, of course, isn't always possible, and the coach who plans ahead usually will find the best possible substitute. He may be able to rely upon a fellow teacher who has a basic knowledge of football in terms of formations and basic patterns as well as defensive alignments and coverages. Often, a former teammate or a former player who has a knowledge of the coach's program will perform excellently and volunteer to see the most important opponent several times. Frequently, there are former college or professional players in the community who would be happy to return to the game through this avenue of observation. Whether it is a member of the coach's regular staff or a volunteer, this is the basic outline he should follow:

1. Study the scouting forms and refer to them as a check on what to look for.
2. Be seated 45 minutes before game time on visiting or highest side about the 30-yard line.
3. View every play only as an opportunity to gain certain information. If you're enjoying the game, you're not conscientiously doing your job.
4. Report must be definite. Omit anything that has not been checked. Make sure you purchase a program.
5. During warm-up, memorize names and numbers of backs and ends who'll start the game.
6. Don't try to write too much.
7. List details you are looking for, in order of importance.
8. After game, check your notes before leaving your seat. You will have time while waiting for statistics.
9. Anything that isn't clear should be straightened out while the game is still fresh in your mind.
10. List the points to be checked at the next game.
11. Fill out Scouting Report as soon as possible after the game.
12. Include newspaper clipping of game, give any play-by-play account, if possible.

SCOUTING OPPONENT'S DEFENSE

In order to make an effective analysis of the opponent, film analysis and on-the-scene scouting should provide answers relative to both offense and defense. These defensive elements must be determined to properly prepare a team's offensive strategy:

1. Base defense
2. Any alternate defenses
3. Base coverages
4. Alternate coverages
5. Short yardage defenses
6. Long yardage or prevent defenses
7. Goal line defense
8. Major stunts
9. Pass-rush ratio

10. Pass-rush contain
11. Specific personnel, that is, their techniques and ability
12. Defensive analysis
    a. Down and distance analysis—normal, long, short
    b. Field position
13. Punt defense—on third or fourth downs, rush or return
14. Kick off coverage—the distance of the kick, crossing men, safeties, and best coverage men
15. Plays that have hurt their defense
    a. Specific runs
    b. Specific passes
16. Strongest phases of their defense
17. Weakest phases of their defense
18. Analysis of their defensive philosophy and thinking
19. Evaluation of their defensive attitude
20. General suggestions offensively, or the answer to one of the two most important scouting questions, "How can we win?"

SCOUTING THE OPPONENT'S OFFENSE

The following are questions that should be answered for the benefit of the defense, based on what the opponent's offense is in the habit of doing:

1. Their base offense
2. Their goal line offense
3. Short yardage offense
4. Primary formations
5. Six best running plays
6. Four best pass plays
7. Offensive analysis
    a. 1-10 tendency—run or pass
    b. Run downs
    c. Pass downs
8. Strong phases of offense
9. Weak phases of offense
10. Punt formation
11. Second and third down punt formations and any runs from them
12. Kick-off formation
13. Pass or run plays from field goal formation
14. Things that have hurt them, such as stunts, rotation
15. Key personnel

16. Offensive team attitude and successes
17. Suggestions defensively or the answer to the question, "What must we stop?"

It is imperative to seek, and respect, the scout's opinions and recommendations for attacking the opponent both offensively and defensively. It is very easy to become so bogged down with facts and figures that the scout never has the opportunity to give his own opinion of what the best procedures should be. Most of what the opponent does is very obvious; it is the not-so-obvious or well-concealed attacks that require preparation to realize the most success.

The high school coach may not have the personnel or funds to carry out the scouting procedures outlined. It is quite possible that he will have to depend upon one man to scout both the offense and defense of the opponent. In that event, he can follow a much more simplified approach which should include these facts:

1. Huddle, shift, cadence
2. Remarks on offensive and defense personnel; best players, possible worst players
3. General remarks on offense; multiple formations, basic plays, passing formations, short yardage plays.
4. General remarks on defense; basic defensive alignment, overshifts, deep secondary coverage, goal line, short yardage.
5. Strongest and weakest phases of opponent's offense and defense.
6. Recommendations for offense and defense that will be effective against opponent.

This information, coupled with the staff's previously acquired knowledge, should be enough to prepare a squad for a particular opponent. Remember, too much information can be dangerous; the only information that is important is what can be used effectively. A coach should be sure that the least knowledgeable assistant or player knows what he is talking about.

GENERAL SCOUTING PROCEDURES

1. All coaches should check with the in-office film man on arrangements to obtain the required films and on the times that they will be available for study. Films should not be kept too long. If two or more persons are scheduled to work together, it is important to block out the necessary time for effective use of the film.

2. Check with other staff members who are assigned to order newspapers from the communities of upcoming opponents. Newspapers generally write factual information regarding injuries and other information that can be interpreted and integrated into the overall scouting report.

3. One man on the staff should be in charge of all the necessary scouting supplies so that they can be contained in one central file; each coach, therefore, does not have to be responsible for all of the various necessary forms and information.

4. Those in charge of scouting should arrange with the athletic department secretary during the summer for travel arrangements and reservations, thus avoiding the fall rush of business. This includes making use of school cars, etc.

5. If at all possible, the scout should return to the home school immediately following the game he views. Copies of his written report should be ready by 7 p.m. on Sunday following a Saturday game. The scout should be prepared to undergo a thorough question-and-answer period between 7:30 and 10 p.m. on Sunday. The written reports for squad members should not be distributed until Monday evening, but they should be completed on Sunday so that work will not interfere with the Monday schedule. The reports for the squad should be distributed at the Monday evening training table.

Taking the Play-by-Play

Each scout should take an ample supply of blank report forms on his assignment. The offensive play-by-play is a very difficult assignment, and any previous knowledge of the opposition that he can acquire will be very useful. If the defensive scout or a volunteer person is available to keep up with the down and distance and hash marks and play gain, it will greatly aid the scout recording the information. We don't usually require a defensive play-by-play, but we do require a summary of defenses in normal long and short yardage situations. A scout should have specific opinions and a "feel" for the team scouted rather than just volumes of information. There are coaches who are often suspected of weighing the reports to determine the efficiency of the report! It is not the size of the report that counts, it is what it contains.

The scout report contents are transmitted by the appropriate coaches to the players, and the squad members additionally receive this written information:

1. Title sheet—general information
2. Personnel (Offensive and Defensive)
3. Formations (basic)

4. Favorite runs vs. our defense (1 page) Favorite tendencies
5. Favorite passes vs. our defense (1 page) Best receivers
6. Basic defenses
   a. Goal line and short yardage
7. Kicking game

Here are some tips to be followed in the coach-scout relationship:

Offensive scouting—Don't ask the scout too much. Ask him to supply basic information concerning alignment, basic action of the backfield, any key players. Don't expect the inexperienced scout to obtain a lot of the opponent's different tendencies. He either is incapable of gathering the information or his conclusions very well might not be valid.

Defensive scouting—A coach can consider it a major accomplishment if the scout determines the opponent's alignment—whether it is an odd or even defense, and if a three- or four-deep coverage is used. That information, along with key personnel, will give a coach a sound basis for setting up his attack.

Kicking game—These reports should be as simple and as easily read as possible. However, it is extremely important to have full knowledge of an opponent's capabilities from both a punting and return standpoint. A thorough understanding of when and how a team makes fullest use of its kicking abilities will assist a team in setting up its game strategy and approach to its own kicking game.

Computerized Scouting

With the development of new and improved computers and other time-saving devices, we are examining the feasibility of a sophisticated scouting system both from the efficiency and financial points of view. The most highly developed computer programs have been developed in professional football. Computer programs produce reports for prospect scouting and game preparation. The first effort by professional teams in the National Football League to use computer-produced reports in the valuation of college prospects was initiated in 1963 by the Los Angeles Rams, the San Francisco 49'ers and the Dallas Cowboys.

The two-scout system is advantageous because the scout responsible for defense can assist the scout who is responsible for offense. There are only so many seconds between plays to gather all of the necessary information, and it is virtually impossible without assistance. In this case, the scout responsible for each area should indicate to the other exactly what he wants him to look for. After the entire information is gathered, the scout should compile it immediately and begin formulating answers to questions that he will get from the coaching staff. Once again, the more a scout is prepared before a game, the easier it will be for him to make his analysis at its conclusion.

We believe that it is important to select a scout who can see several of the opponents so a continuity is developed and comparisons can be drawn. A coach must realize that his scout probably will not see the home team play because of his primary duties. In this case, he should attend spring practice, early fall practice, and actually go through scouting procedures during a scrimmage of his home team.

The head coach should make a thorough evaluation of the opponents before outlining to the scout exactly what is expected of him. A head coach who is well organized and understands his opponents will have the necessary information on most of the teams he plays, so the scout merely will be a vehicle for him to substantiate what he already knows or to determine if any new wrinkles have been introduced by the opposition.

SUMMARY

We have attempted to answer two basic questions with the material contained in this book: (1) How to drill for agility, tackling, and techniques in the three defensive areas (linemen-linebackers-defensive backs); (2) The presentation of sets, rules, functions, stunts and coverages for the major even defenses that are used today. We in no way consider any of this material as written in stone. It is our hope that we have given you enough information for you to develop an even defensive look that best fits your personnel and situation. No matter what defense you choose, your attitude and enthusiasm are still keys to its success. You must sell your players on the defense. If they believe they can be a better team with an even defense, you have won half the battle. Positive salesmanship will be a major factor.

INDEX

DATE DUE

JUN 1 2 1984	NO 2 ~ ~	
OC 1 '84	FE 15 '96	
AG 1 '85	JAN 1 7 1997	
SE 5 '85		
DE 3 '86	OC 20 '97	
AP 11 '88	MR 3 '98	
SE 6 '89	OC 1 5 1998	
MR 7 '90	AUG 02 1999	
MR 28 '90	MY 25 '99	
AP 24 '90		
FE 19 '92		
MEND JAN		
NO 4 '92		
DE 1 ?		
JY 25 '93		
SE 13 '93		

DEMCO 38-297